LEARN TO Quilt-As-You-Go

14 PROJECTS YOU CAN FINISH FAST

Gudrun Erla

Learn to Quilt-As-You-Go:
14 Projects You Can Finish Fast

Martingale®
19021 120th Ave. NE, Ste. 102
Bothell, WA 98011-9511 USA
ShopMartingale.com

Printed in China
20 19 18 17 16 15   8 7 6 5 4 3 2 1

Library of Congress Cataloging-in-Publication Data is available upon request.

ISBN: 978-1-60468-489-6

MISSION STATEMENT

Dedicated to providing quality products and service to inspire creativity.

CREDITS

PUBLISHER AND CHIEF VISIONARY OFFICER
Jennifer Erbe Keltner

EDITORIAL DIRECTOR
Karen Costello Soltys

ACQUISITIONS EDITOR
Karen M. Burns

TECHNICAL EDITOR
Laurie Baker

COPY EDITOR
Marcy Heffernan

DESIGN DIRECTOR
Paula Schlosser

PHOTOGRAPHER
Brent Kane

PRODUCTION MANAGER
Regina Girard

COVER AND INTERIOR DESIGNER
Adrienne Smitke

ILLUSTRATOR
Lisa Lauch

Contents

Introduction

I've never been called the most patient person in any group. As a matter of fact, I like to get things done quickly and efficiently with great results so I can move on to the next project. My list of projects is of course endless; there are so many things I want to try, make, and experience.

Early in my quilting life, when I had just started designing my own patterns, I began playing with the quilt-as-you-go method. I liked the idea of piecing something and quilting it at the same time so I could actually finish a project instead of having it sitting around as a quilt top waiting for the magical quilting part. The fact that I had three kids (two under the age of two!), two quilt shops to run, and aerobics classes to teach four nights a week as well, may have played a big part in me choosing to give that method a try. I didn't have much extra time for sewing.

That's how my first quilt-as-you-go patterns were born. Once quilters tried one of the patterns, they demanded more. They loved being able to get a little project done from start to finish in just a few hours. More and more patterns led to me writing books filled with quilt-as-you-go projects.

I love challenges, so finding different techniques to accomplish a certain look or making things easier and more accurate with the quilt-as-you-go method has always been fun for me. For this method, you start with the whole piece of backing fabric and batting basted together and then piece the quilt top through all the layers as you go. Because of that, I don't recommend making quilts larger than about 50" to 60" with this method. But there are so many projects you can make even though you can't make a bed quilt. Make a bed runner, pillows, table toppers, table runners, place mats, and more. Quilt-as-you-go projects are great for decorating your house or to give as gifts.

This book will take you through the techniques of the quilt-as-you-go method step by step (beginning on page 66), so even if you've never tried quilting as you go, you can be successful right out of the gate. And if you're already familiar with the basic techniques, you'll still find something new here. In this book, I wanted to tackle another challenge—making things look like they're done a certain way even when they really aren't. For example, while there isn't a way to do curved piecing or inset seams when quilting as you go, I've found some great ways to make quilts have the illusion of curves. Or to have the look of set-in seams. I've also added prairie points into seams to add dimension to some of the projects.

Look for the icons in the table of contents as well as behind the page numbers, for a quick reference about the shape and type of techniques used for each project. First, we start with basic squares and rectangles. Then we move on to triangles, strips, prairie points, and curves. I hope you enjoy making the little projects in the book and add to your set of quiltmaking skills in the process.

Let's Dish
PLACE MATS

FINISHED PLACE MATS: 13" x 18"

Strip-pieced place mats are quick and easy to assemble, yet they can really enhance the look of your dining area. They make great gifts too. For a coordinated but not identical set, randomly select different-colored and different-width strips as you go.

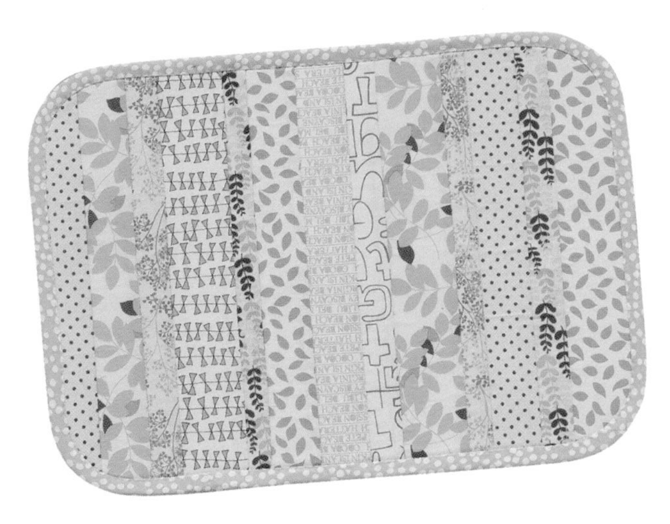

MATERIALS

Yardage is based on 42"-wide fabric and is sufficient to make 6 place mats.

8 assorted fat quarters (18" x 21") for top
⅔ yard of coordinating print for binding
1⅜ yards of fabric for backing
1 yard of 45"-wide batting or 2¼ yards of 20"-wide heavyweight interfacing*
Scrap of freezer paper (optional)

** I used CRAF-TEX Plus interfacing from Bosal, which is fusible on both sides. You can also use precut rectangular place mats with rounded corners from Bosal.*

CUTTING

From the batting or interfacing, cut:
6 rectangles, 13" x 18"

From *each* of the 8 fat quarters, cut*:
3 strips, 2½" x 18" (24 total)
3 strips, 2" x 18" (24 total)
3 strips, 1½" x 18" (24 total)
2 strips, 1¼" x 18" (16 total)

From the backing fabric, cut:
3 strips, 13" x 42"; crosscut into 6 rectangles, 13" x 18"

From the *bias* of the coordinating print for binding, cut:
Enough 2½"-wide strips to make a 432"-long strip when pieced together

**See "Quick Cutting" below for more information on cutting the fat quarters.*

Quick Cutting

To speed up the cutting process, stack as many fat quarters as you're comfortable cutting at the same time, aligning the raw edges. Cut the strips from the short side of the fat-quarter stack.

ASSEMBLING THE PLACE MATS

Sew with right sides together using a ¼" seam allowance.

1. Refer to "Baste the Backing and Batting Together" (page 68) to attach a batting rectangle to the wrong side of each backing rectangle using your favorite method. If you're using the precut place-mat forms, follow the manufacturer's

instructions to fuse a form to the wrong side of each backing rectangle. Trim the backing fabric even with the batting, interfacing, or form.

2. Choose any fat-quarter strip and lay it right side up on the far-left side of a prepared batting or interfacing rectangle, aligning the raw edge of the strip with the batting or interfacing edge. The strip should completely cover the width of the rectangle. Don't worry if it extends past the rectangle; the excess will be trimmed later. Select a strip cut from a different fabric and of a different width, and layer it on top of the first strip, right sides together, aligning the edges on the right edge of the first strip; pin in place. Sew along the aligned raw edges of the strips through all the layers; press the strip open.

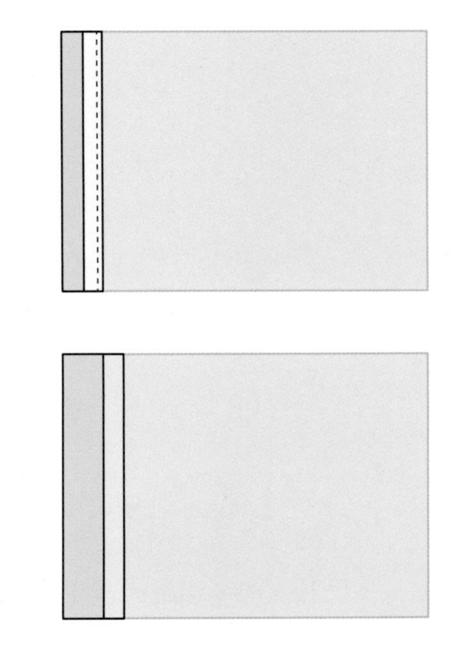

3. Referring to step 2 and the illustration above right, select another strip from a different fabric and of a different width and sew it to the right edge of the previous strip in the same manner; press the strip open. Continue adding strips to the batting/interfacing rectangle in this manner until the rectangle is covered, pressing each new strip open before adding the next strip.

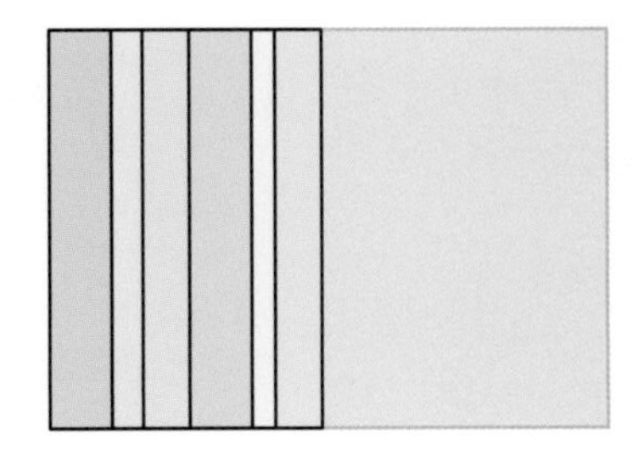

4. Flip the place mat over and trim any excess fabric extending beyond the backing and batting/interfacing. For rounded corners on your place mat, trace the corner-cutting pattern below onto freezer paper and cut it out. (If you started with a precut place-mat form with already rounded corners, you can skip this step.) Lay the template on one corner of the place mat and trace the arc. Repeat for all four corners, and then use scissors to cut on the marked lines.

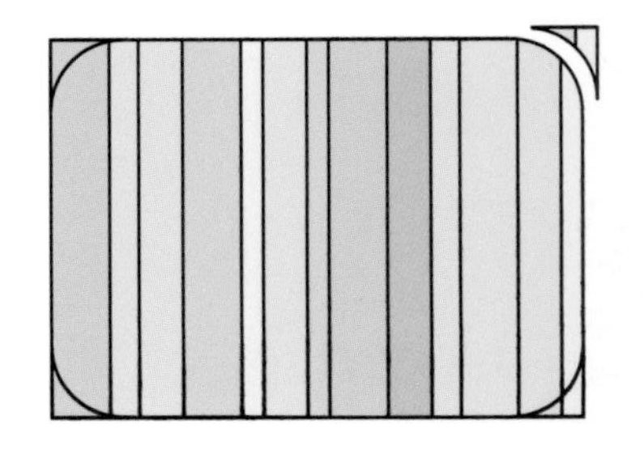

5. Repeat steps 2–4 with the remaining batting or interfacing rectangles, or place-mat forms.

FINISHING

Refer to "Bias Binding" (page 78) to join the 2½"-wide binding strips into one long strip and use it to bind the edges of each place mat.

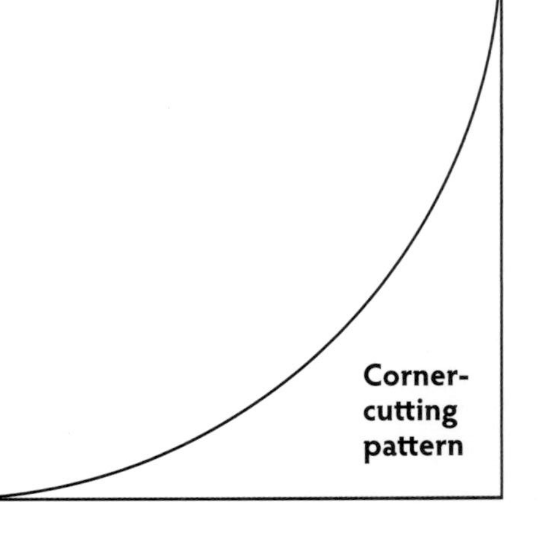

Scraptastic
COASTERS

FINISHED COASTERS: 4½" x 4½"

Perfect for the family room or anywhere friends and family are hanging out, these coasters are super quick to make. Pair them with a nice bottle of wine for a thoughtful hostess or housewarming gift.

MATERIALS

Materials are sufficient to make 4 coasters.

⅜ yard *total* of assorted-print scraps for tops
1 fat quarter (18" x 21") of coordinating solid for binding
1 fat eighth (9" x 21") of fabric for backing
5" x 20" piece of batting
5" x 5" square of freezer paper or tracing paper

CUTTING

From the backing fabric, cut:
1 rectangle, 5" x 20"

From the assorted-print scraps, cut:
Approximately 28 strips, at least 1¼" x 8' (you may use more or less, depending on the strip widths)

From the *bias* of the coordinating solid, cut:
4 strips, 2¼" x at least 24"

ASSEMBLING THE COASTERS

Sew with right sides together using a ¼" seam allowance.

1. Refer to "Baste the Backing and Batting Together" (page 68) to attach the batting to the wrong side of the backing rectangle using your favorite method.
2. Lay a print strip across the batting diagonally as shown, right side up. Make sure it extends past the top and bottom edges of the batting. Position another strip on top of the first strip, aligning the raw edges along the right edge of the first strip; pin in place. Sew along the right edge of the strips through all layers; press the strip open.

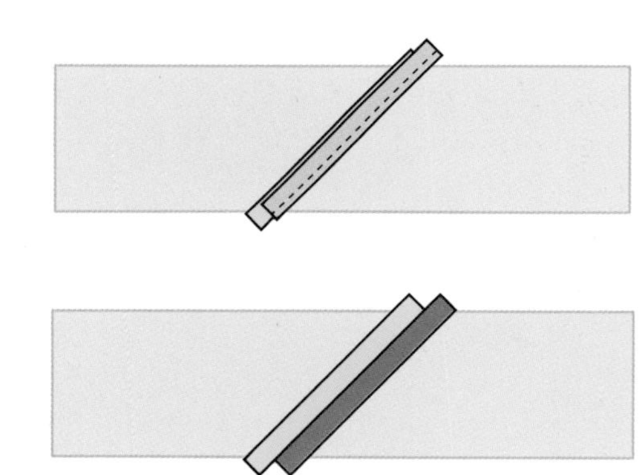

3. Position another print strip on the last strip added, aligning the raw edges on the right edge of the last strip; pin and then sew in place. Press the strip open. Lay a print strip on top of the first strip, aligning the raw edges along the left edge of the first strip; pin and then sew in place. Press the strip open.

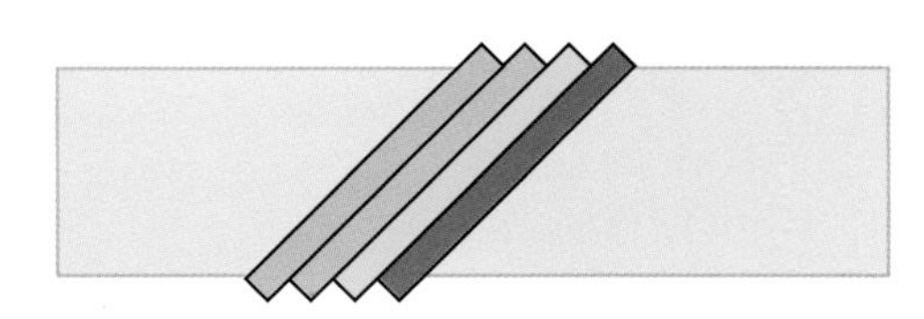

4. Continue adding strips to the right and left sides of the pieced unit until you've completely covered the batting.

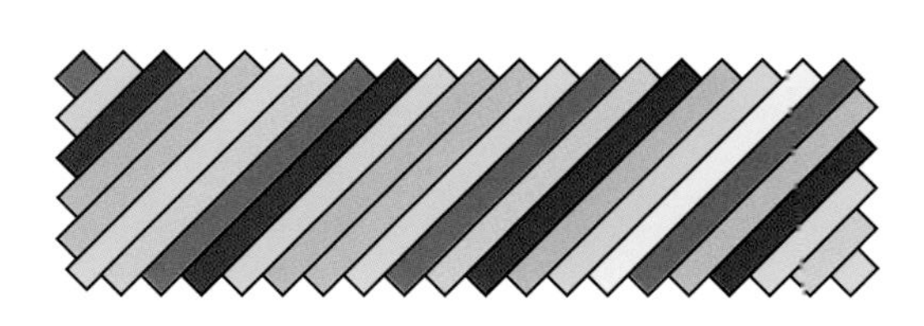

5. Trace the coaster pattern below onto freezer paper or tracing paper and cut it out. Lay the template on the strip-pieced unit, making sure it covers all of the layers; trace around it. Repeat to trace four coaster shapes. Cut out each coaster on the drawn lines.

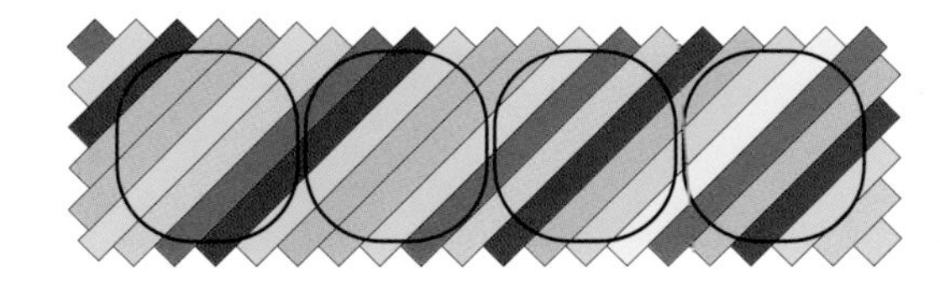

FINISHING

Refer to "Bias Binding" (page 78) to bind each coaster with the solid 2¼"-wide strips. Use the tucked-ends method (page 78) to cut the ends at a 60° angle to join them.

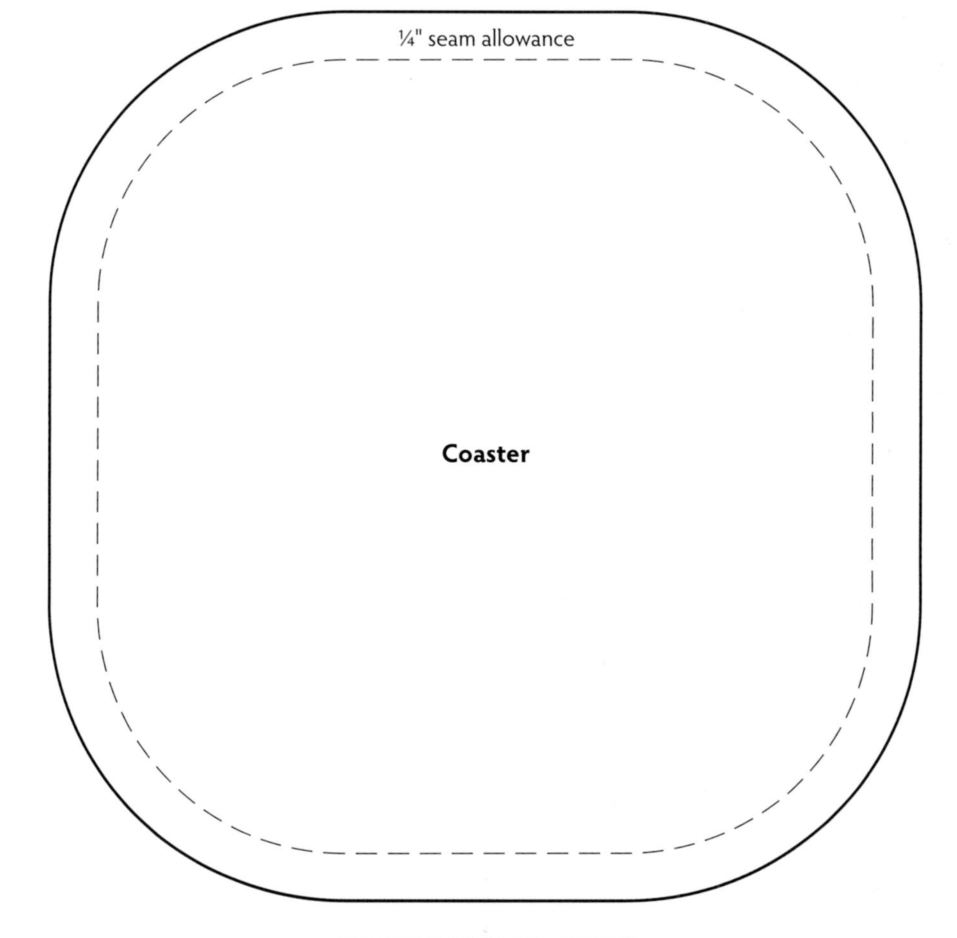

Step It Up
TABLE TOPPER

FINISHED TABLE TOPPER: 24½" x 24½"

Turn a jumbo Courthouse Steps block into a fashionable table topper. Simply choose your three-color fabric combination, and you're good to go.

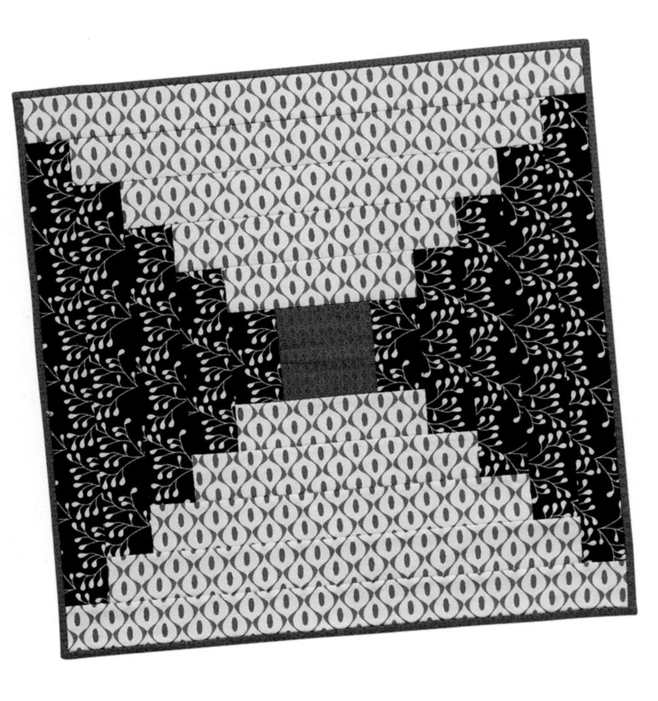

MATERIALS

Yardage is based on 42"-wide fabric.

⅞ yard of red print for center square, backing, and binding
½ yard of white print for top
⅜ yard of black print for top
⅞ yard of batting

CUTTING

From the batting, cut:
1 square, 27" x 27"

From the red print, refer to the illustration below to cut:
1 square, 27" x 27"
1 square, 4½" x 4½"
5 strips, 2½" x 27" (approximately)

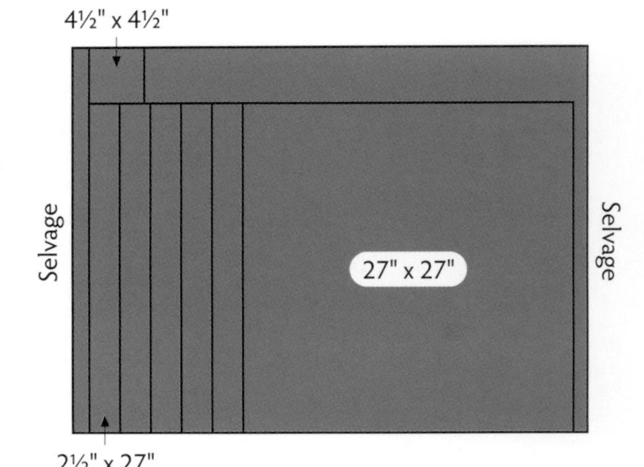

Continued on page 14.

Continued from page 12.

From the black print, cut:
4 strips, 2½" x 42"; crosscut into:
- 2 rectangles, 2½" x 20½"
- 2 rectangles, 2½" x 16½"
- 2 rectangles, 2½" x 12½"
- 2 rectangles, 2½" x 8½"
- 2 rectangles, 2½" x 4½"

From the white print, cut:
5 strips, 2½" x 42"; crosscut into:
- 2 rectangles, 2½" x 24½"
- 2 rectangles, 2½" x 20½"
- 2 rectangles, 2½" x 16½"
- 2 rectangles, 2½" x 12½"
- 2 rectangles, 2½" x 8½"

ASSEMBLING THE TABLE TOPPER

Sew with right sides together using a ¼" seam allowance.

1. Refer to "Baste the Backing and Batting Together" (page 68) to attach the batting square to the wrong side of the red 27" square using your favorite method.
2. Draw lines on the batting through the vertical and horizontal centers to mark the center of the square.

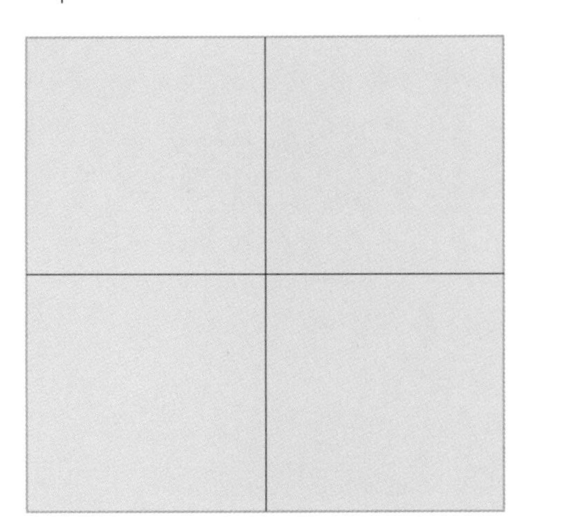

3. Pin the red 4½" square to the center of the batting, right side up. Pin a black 2½" x 4½" rectangle on top of the center square, aligning the top raw edges. Sew along the top edge of the rectangle through all the layers; press the rectangle open. In the same manner, add a black 2½" x 4½" rectangle to the bottom edge of the center square; press the rectangle open.

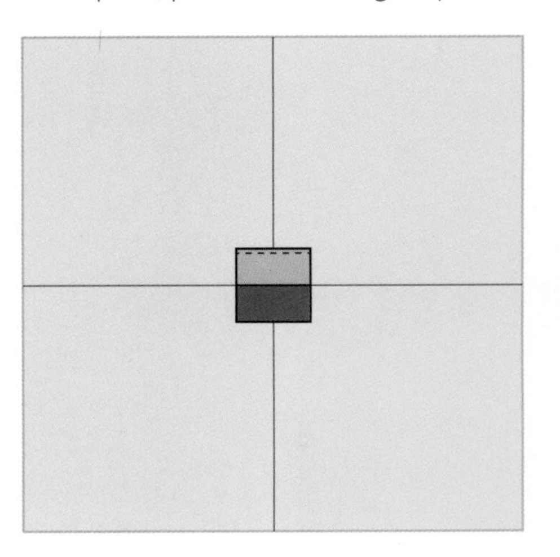

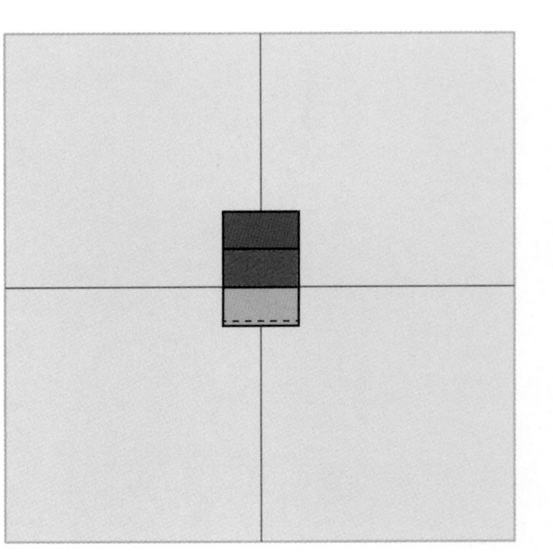

4. Pin and then sew the white 2½" x 8½" rectangles to the sides of the center unit, aligning the raw edges; press the rectangles open.

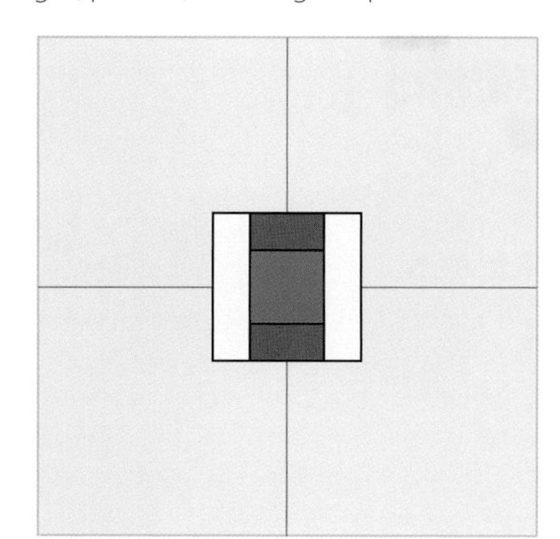

5. Pin and then sew the black 2½" x 8½" rectangles to the top and bottom edges of the center unit; press the rectangles open.

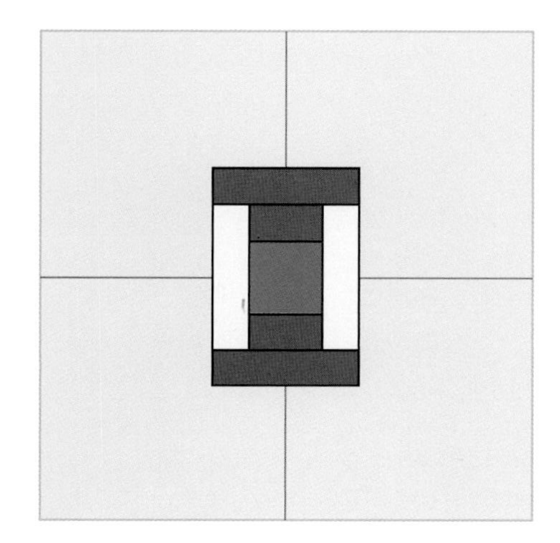

6. Pin and then sew the white 2½" x 12½" rectangles to the sides of the center unit; press the rectangles open.

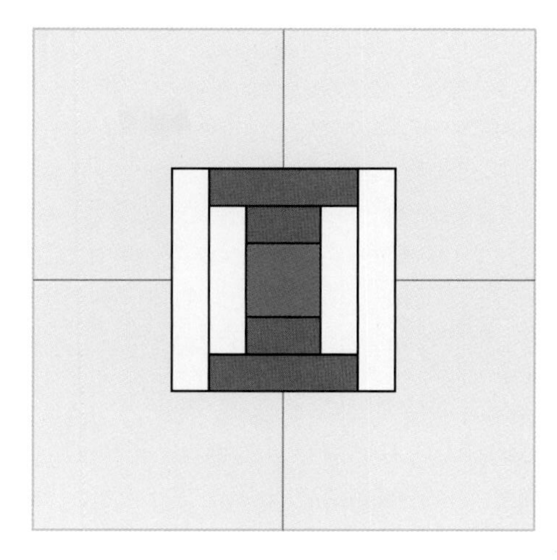

7. Continue adding rectangles to the center unit, working from shortest to longest and alternating the colors so the white rectangles are sewn to the left and right sides and the black rectangles are sewn to the top and bottom edges. Press the rectangles open after each addition.

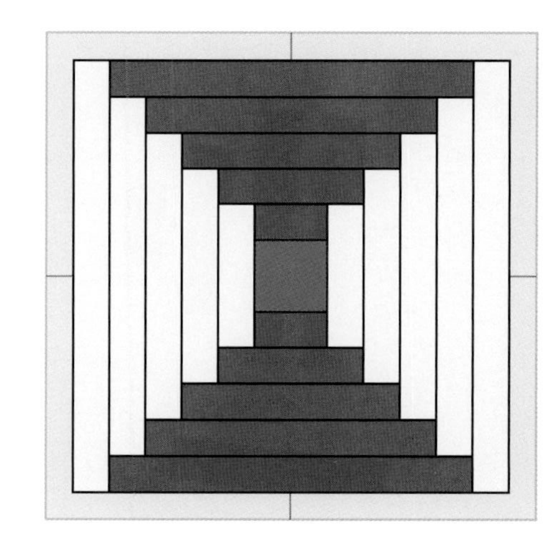

FINISHING

1. Trim the batting and backing even with the topper edges.
2. Refer to "Binding" (page 76) to join the red 2½"-wide strips into one long strip and use it to bind the topper edges.

Stacked Lanterns
TABLE RUNNER

FINISHED TABLE RUNNER: 20½" x 50½"

This project is the perfect marriage of two techniques. Start by making units using traditional piecing methods, and then join the units to the layered batting and backing using the quilt-as-you-go technique.

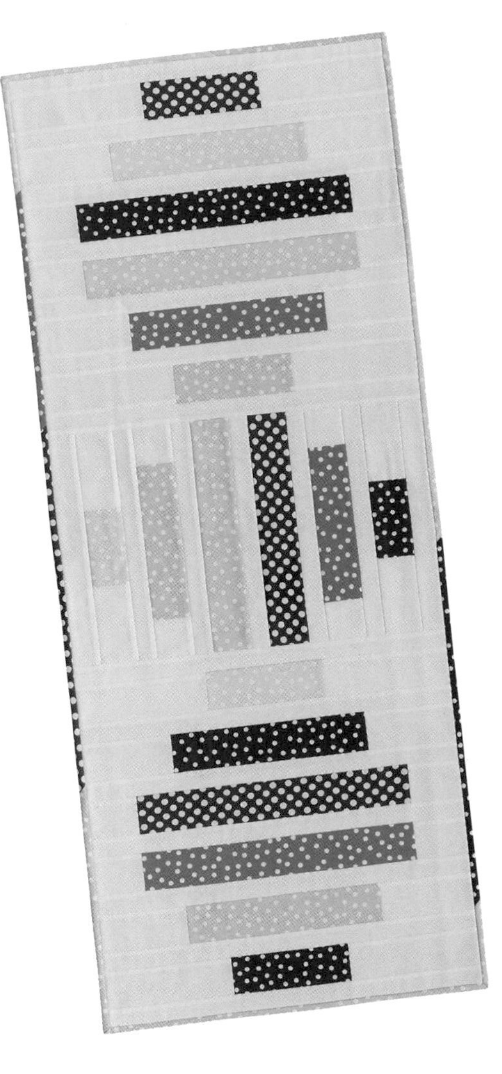

Made by Yvonne Geske

MATERIALS

Yardage is based on 42"-wide fabric.

1 yard of white solid for top
1 fat eighth (9" x 21") *each* of 6 assorted bright prints for top and binding
¾ yard of fabric for backing
23" x 53" piece of batting

CUTTING

From the white solid, cut:

5 strips, 2½" x 42"; crosscut into:
- 8 rectangles, 2½" x 7½"
- 8 rectangles, 2½" x 5½"
- 4 rectangles, 2½" x 4½"
- 8 rectangles, 2½" x 3½"
- 4 squares, 2½" x 2½"

1 strip, 2" x 42"; crosscut into 2 rectangles, 2" x 12½"

9 strips, 1½" x 42"; crosscut into:
- 14 strips, 1½" x 20½"
- 5 strips, 1½" x 12½"

From *each* of the 6 bright prints, cut:

3 strips, 2½" x 21" (18 total). Set aside 1 strip of each color (6 total) for binding. From the remaining strips, cut a *total* of:
- 4 rectangles, 2½" x 14½"
- 2 rectangles, 2½" x 12½"
- 4 rectangles, 2½" x 10½"
- 2 rectangles, 2½" x 8½"
- 4 rectangles, 2½" x 6½"
- 2 rectangles, 2½" x 4½"

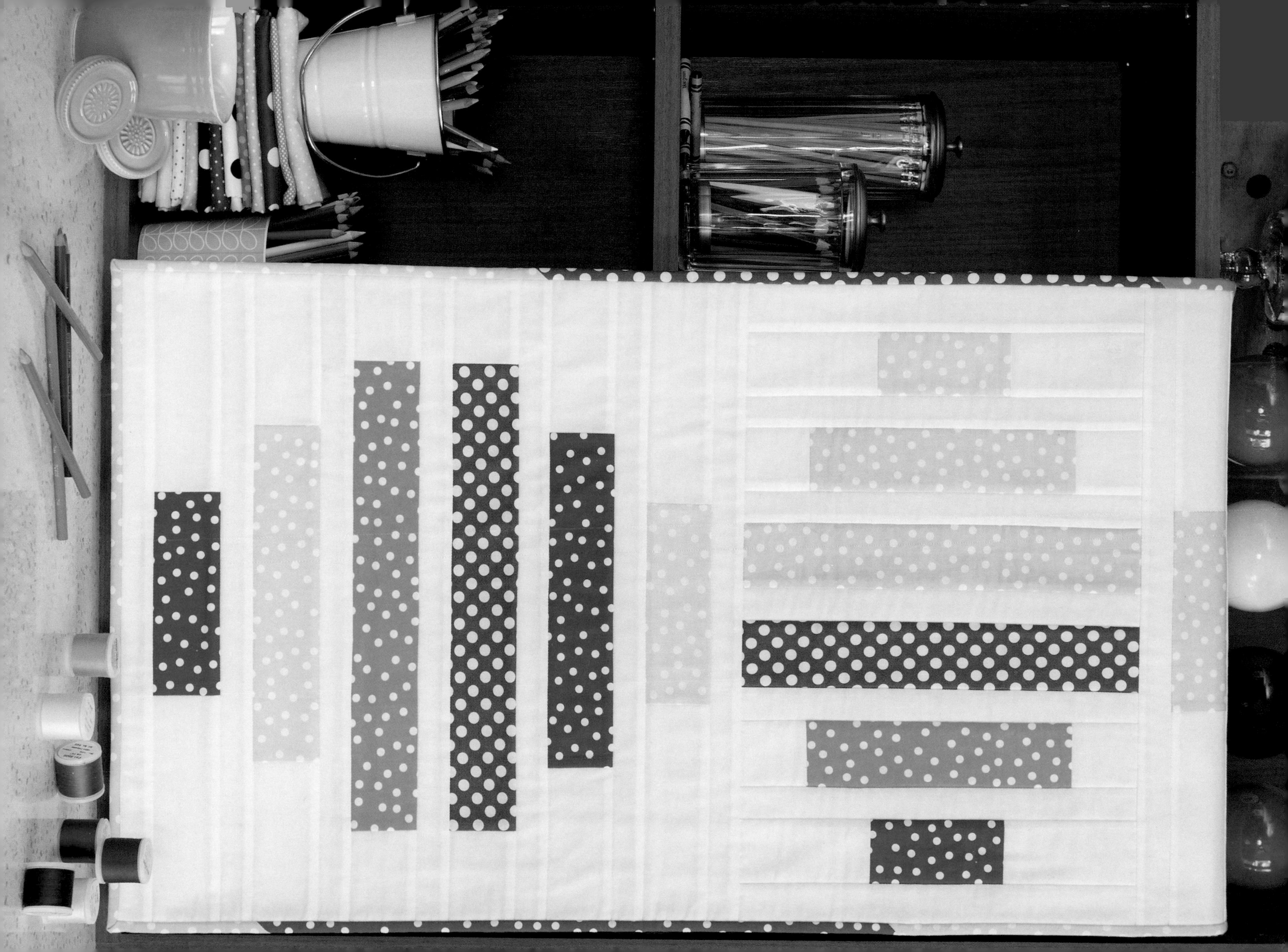

ASSEMBLING THE TABLE RUNNER

Sew with right sides together using a ¼" seam allowance.

1. Sew a white piece to each end of a bright-print rectangle as shown to make units A–E. Make the number indicated for each unit. Press the seam allowances toward the bright prints.

2½" x 2½" | 2½" x 8½" | 2½" x 2½"

Unit A. Make 2.

2½" x 4½" | 2½" x 4½" | 2½" x 4½"

Unit B. Make 2.

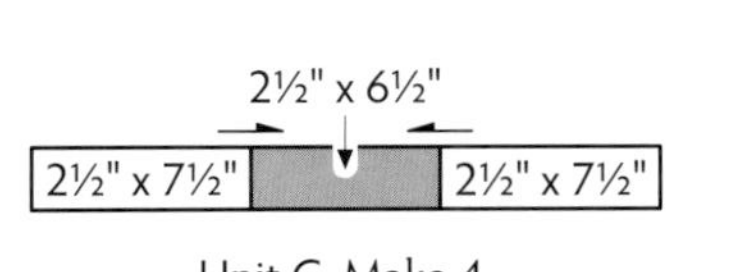

Unit C. Make 4.

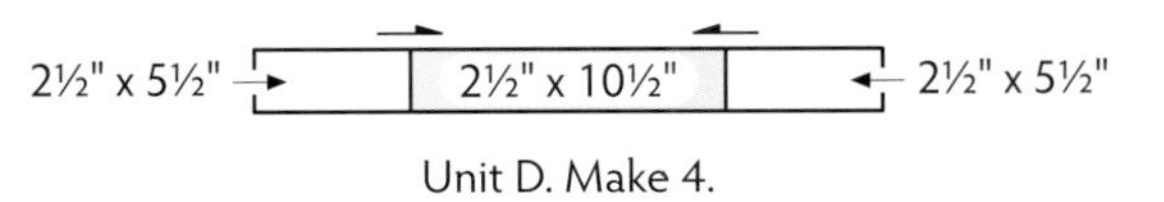

Unit D. Make 4.

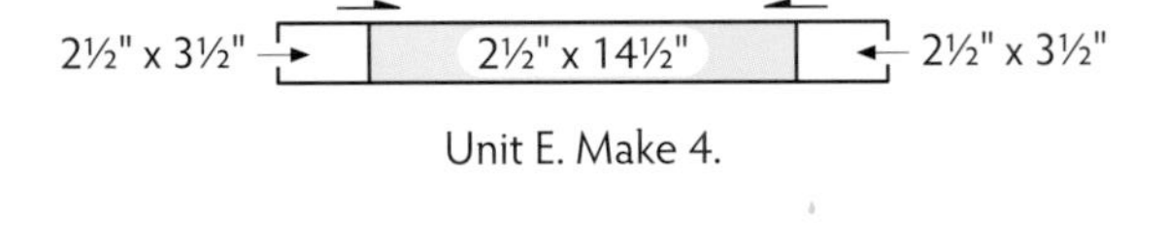

Unit E. Make 4.

2. From the backing fabric, make a piece approximately 23" x 53". Refer to "Baste the Backing and Batting Together" (page 68) to attach the batting to the pieced backing rectangle using your favorite method.

3. Draw a line through the horizontal and vertical centers of the batting. Draw parallel lines 10¼" from each side of the horizontal center line and 6¼" from each side of the vertical center line.

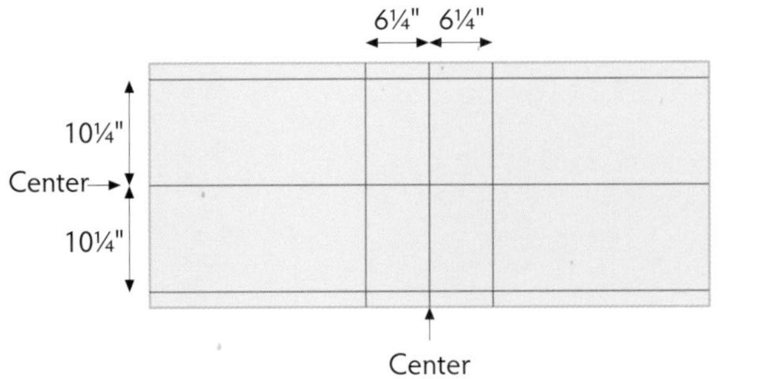

4. Center a white 1½" x 12½" strip on the horizontal line between the two vertical lines, right side up; pin in place.

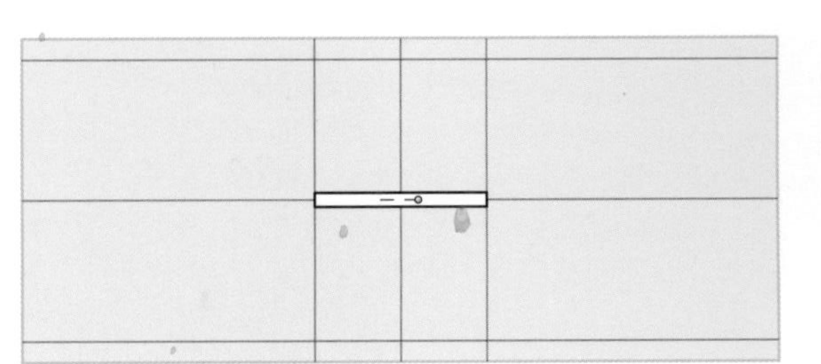

5. Place a bright-print 2½" x 12½" rectangle on top of the white rectangle, right sides together, aligning the raw edges along the top of the white strip; pin in place. Sew along the top edge, stitching through all the layers. Press the print rectangle open. Add another bright-print 2½" x 12½" rectangle to the bottom edge of the white rectangle and press it open.

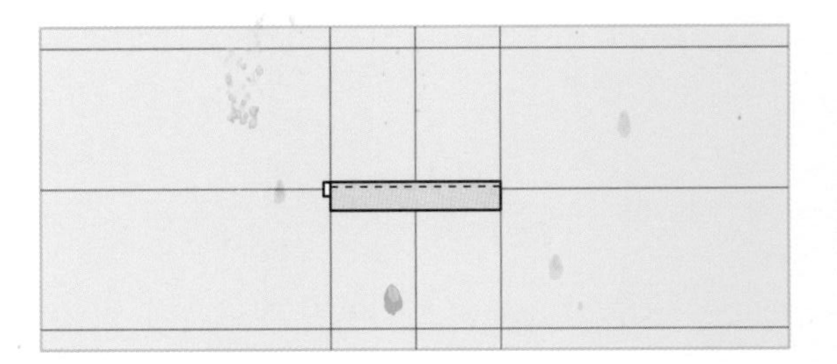

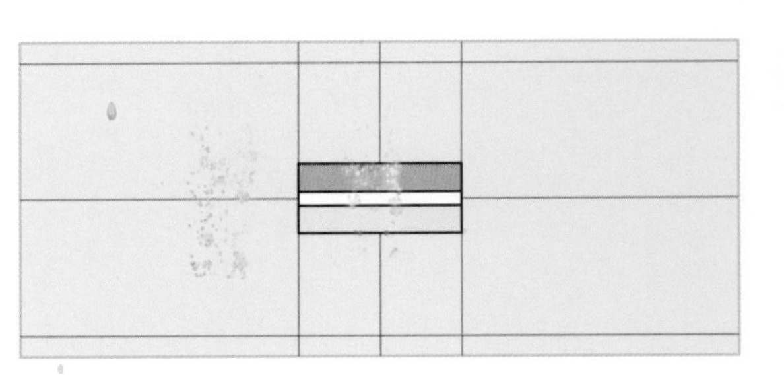

6. Sew a white 1½" x 12½" rectangle to the long raw edge of each of the bright-print rectangles; press it open. Add an A unit to the long raw edge of each white strip; press it open.

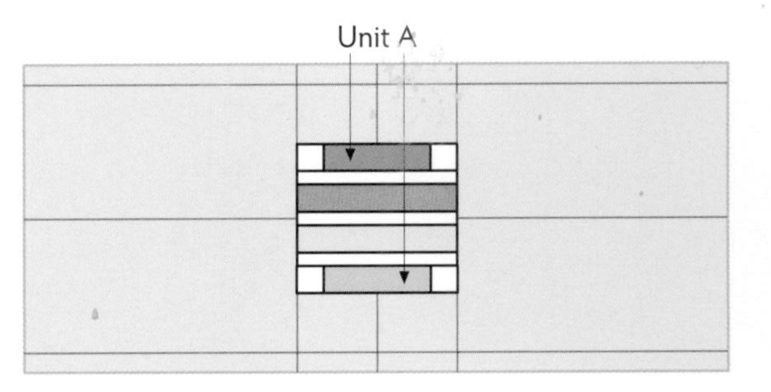

7. Sew a white 1½" x 12½" rectangle to the long raw edge of each A unit; press it open. Add a B unit to the long raw edge of each white rectangle; press it open.

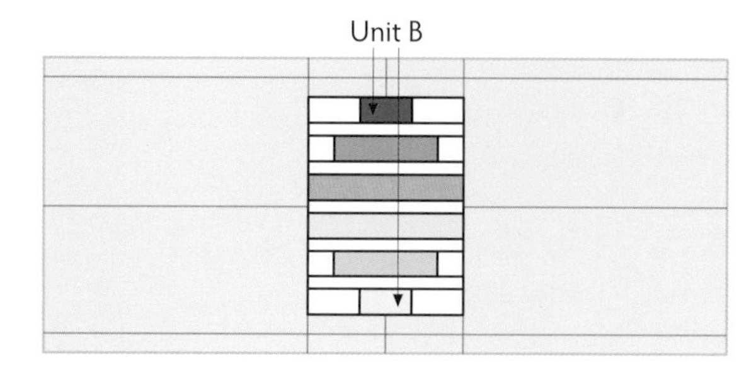

8. Sew a white 2" x 12½" rectangle to the long raw edge of each B unit; press it open.

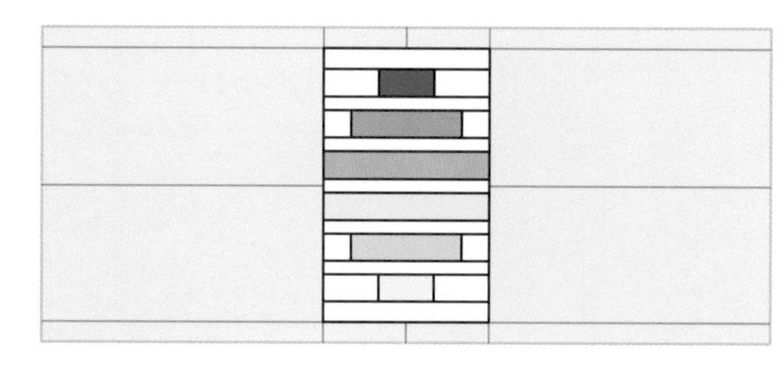

9. Sew a white 1½" x 20½" strip to each side of the center unit; press it open. Add a C unit to the long raw edge of each white strip; press it open.

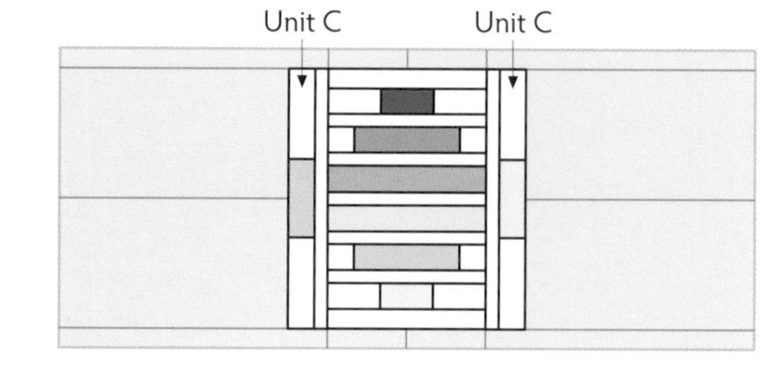

10. Sew a white 1½" x 20½" strip to the long raw edge of each C unit; press it open. Add a D unit to the long raw edge of each white strip; press it open.

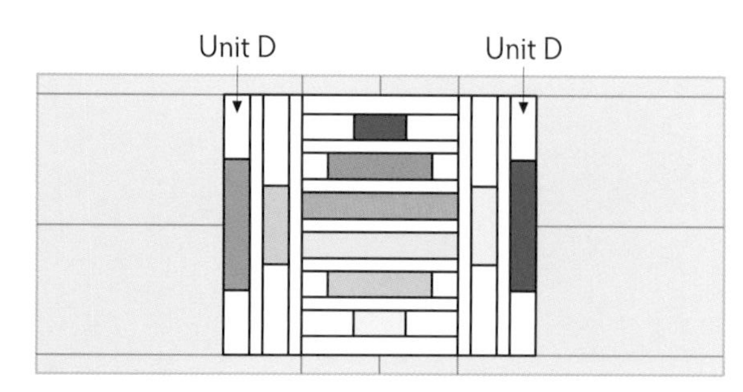

11. Sew a white 1½" x 20½" strip to the long raw edge of each D unit; press it open. Add an E unit to the long raw edge of each white strip; press it open.

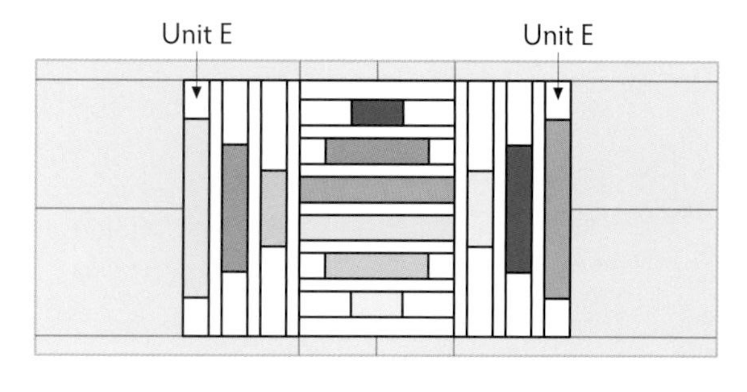

12. In the same manner as established, add the remaining E, D, and C units to the left- and right-hand sides of the stitched piece as shown, separating each pieced unit with a white 1½" x 20½" strip. Press each piece open after stitching it in place. End with a white strip.

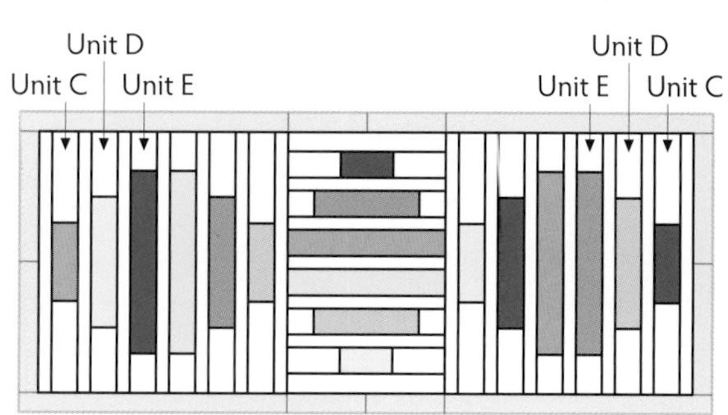

FINISHING

1. Trim the batting and backing even with the runner-top edges.
2. Refer to "Binding" (page 76) to join the six bright-print 2½" x 21" strips into one long strip and use it to bind the runner edges.

Sienna Sunrise
TOPPER

FINISHED TOPPER: 24½" x 30½"

Inspired by the sunrises in Sienna, Italy, the gradation of warm colors used in this topper looks especially stunning when set off with black accents.

MATERIALS

Yardage is based on 42"-wide fabric.

¾ yard of black solid for top and binding
⅓ yard of red solid for top
¼ yard of dark-orange solid for top
1 fat quarter (18" x 21") of light-orange solid for top
1 fat eighth (9" x 21") of gold solid for top
1 fat eighth of yellow solid for top
⅞ yard of fabric for backing
27" x 33" piece of batting

CUTTING

From the backing fabric, cut:
1 rectangle, 27" x 33"

From the black solid, cut:
2 strips, 4⅞" x 42"; crosscut into 10 squares, 4⅞" x 4⅞". Cut each square in half diagonally to yield 20 triangles.
3 strips, 2½" x 42"
1 rectangle, 4½" x 10½"

From the yellow solid, cut:
2 rectangles, 2½" x 4½"
2 rectangles, 2½" x 10½"

From the gold solid, cut:
2 rectangles, 2½" x 8½"
2 rectangles, 2½" x 14½"

From the light-orange solid, cut:
2 rectangles, 2½" x 12½"
2 rectangles, 2½" x 18½"

From the dark-orange solid, cut:
2 rectangles, 2½" x 16½"
2 rectangles, 2½" x 22½"

From the red solid, cut:
2 rectangles, 2½" x 20½"
2 rectangles, 2½" x 26½"

ASSEMBLING THE TOPPER

Sew with right sides together using a ¼" seam allowance.

1. Refer to "Baste the Backing and Batting Together" (page 68) to attach the batting to the wrong side of the backing rectangle using your favorite method.

2. Draw lines on the batting through the vertical and horizontal centers to mark the rectangle center. Pin the black 4½" x 10½" rectangle to the center of the batting, right side up.

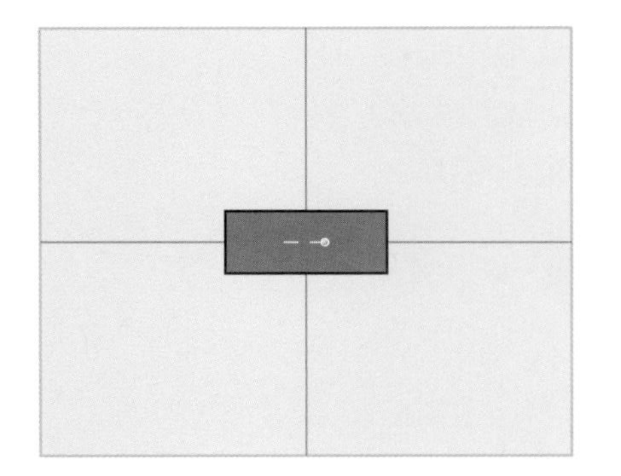

3. Place a yellow 2½" x 4½" rectangle on top of the center rectangle, aligning the short raw edges with the right edge of the rectangle. Sew along the right edge of the rectangles through all the layers; press the yellow rectangle open. In the same manner, add a yellow 2½" x 4½" rectangle to the left edge of the center rectangle; press the rectangle open.

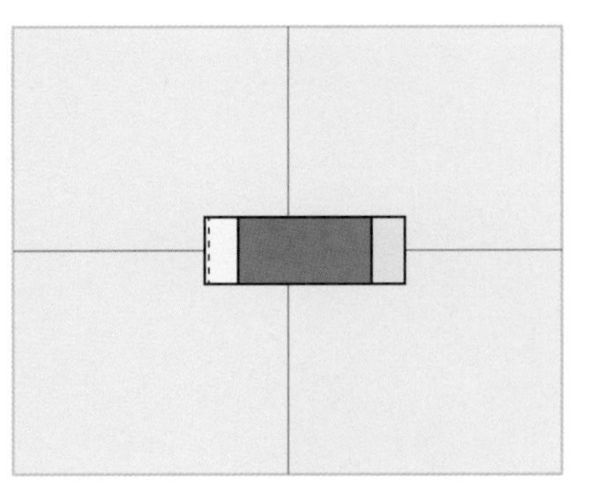

4. Center the yellow 2½" x 10½" rectangles on the top and bottom edges of the black rectangle. The ends of the yellow rectangles should extend past the black rectangle ¼"; pin the rectangles in place. Sew along the top and bottom edges. Press the rectangles open.

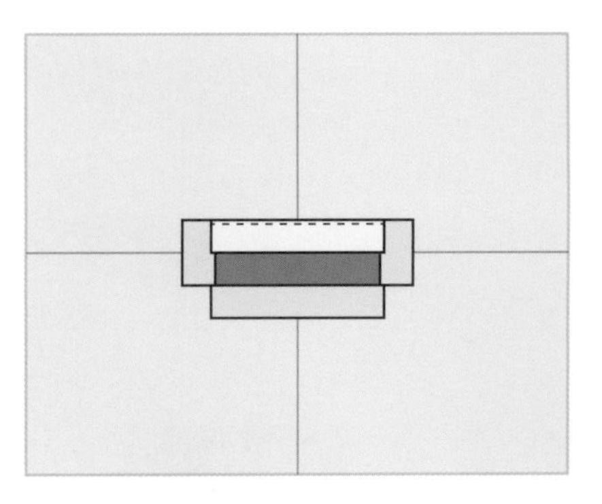

5. Refer to "Adding Triangles to Corners" (page 70) to lay your ruler on the stitched unit, aligning the ¼" line of the ruler with one corner of the black rectangle. Move the ruler around until you can position the 45° line on the ruler with the seam of the black rectangle. Draw a line ¼" from the corner of the rectangle as shown. Repeat for the remaining three corners.

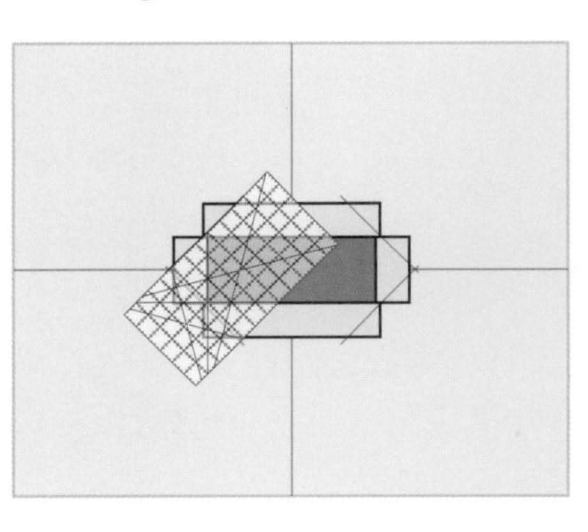

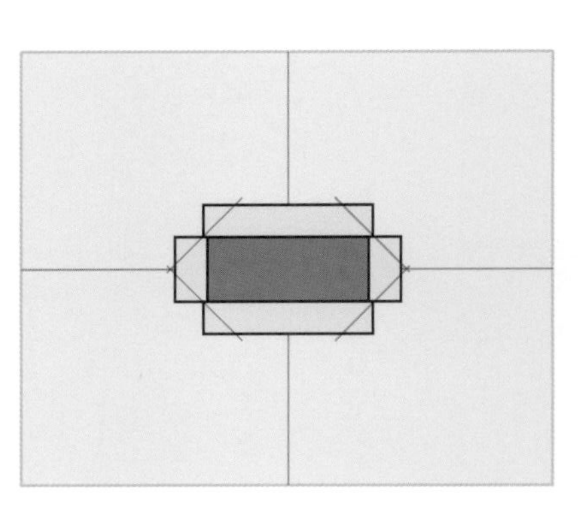

6. Lay black triangles on opposite corners of the black center rectangle, aligning the long edges of the triangles with the drawn lines. Center the triangles so that the triangle tips extend past the yellow rectangles an equal distance on each side; pin in place. Sew along the long edge of each triangle. Trim the excess yellow fabric even with the long edge of each triangle; press the triangles open. Repeat on the opposite corners of the black rectangle.

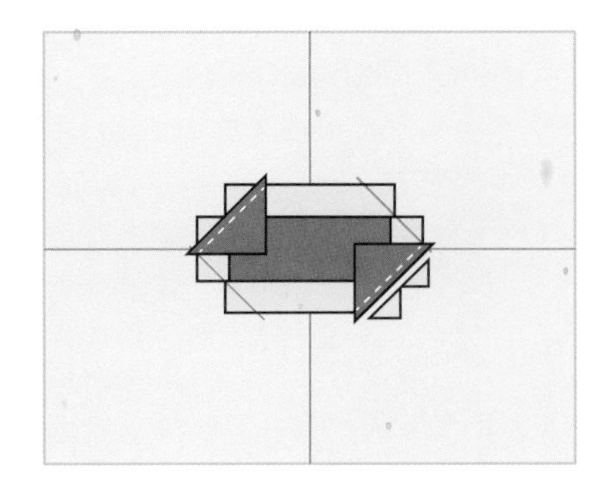

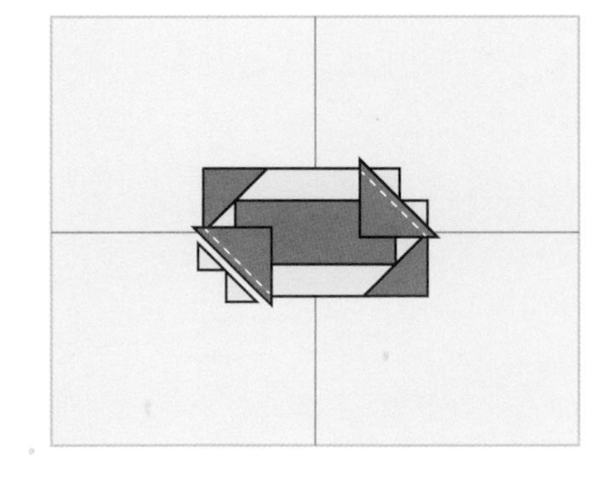

7. Refer to steps 3 and 4 to add the gold rectangles to the pieced unit.

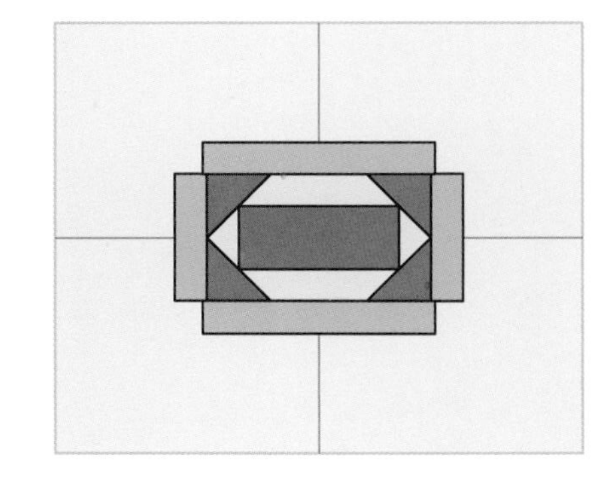

8. Refer to steps 5 and 6 to add black triangles to the corners of the pieced unit.

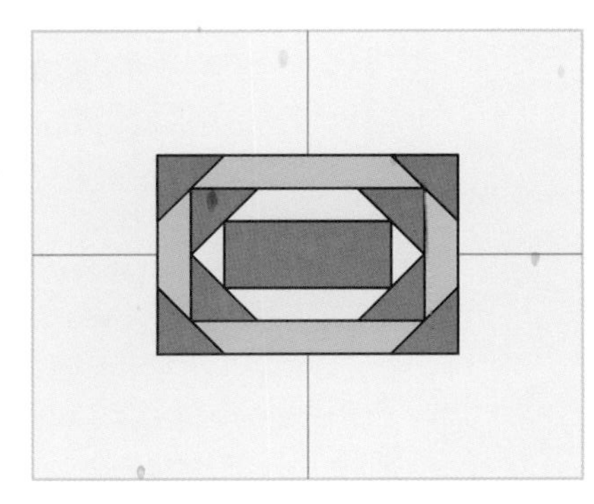

9. Continue in this manner to sew the light-orange, dark-orange, and red rectangles to the pieced unit, adding black triangles to the corners after each round of rectangles has been added.

FINISHING

1. Trim the batting and backing even with the topper edges.
2. Refer to "Binding" (page 76) to join the black 2½"-wide strips into one long strip and use it to bind the topper edges.

Alternate Colorway

For a different look, make the triangles from various prints while keeping the background color uniform. You'll need a total of ⅞ yard of fabric for the background and binding, plus scraps for the triangles and the center rectangle.

Winging It
TABLE RUNNER

FINISHED TABLE RUNNER: 13½" x 53"

Don't let the points fool you. Just follow the lines to easily stitch this runner together in no time flat.

Made by Yvonne Geske

MATERIALS

Yardage is based on 42"-wide fabric.

½ yard of white print for background
½ yard of large-scale pink print for border
1 fat quarter (18" x 21") of small-scale pink print for center diamond and triangles
1 fat eighth (9" x 21") of dark-pink tone on tone for center diamond border and triangles
⅜ yard of multicolored stripe for binding
¾ yard of fabric for backing
15" x 55" piece of batting
Freezer paper

CUTTING

Before you begin cutting, trace the triangle and diamond patterns on pages 28 and 29 onto the dull side of a piece of freezer paper and cut them out. Refer to the cutting instructions below to iron each shape, shiny side down, to the right side of the appropriate fabric; cut out the shape and remove the freezer paper from the fabric. Each freezer-paper shape can be used multiple times.

From the white print, cut:
2 strips, 7½" x 42"; crosscut into 16 rectangles, 3½" x 7½"

From the small-scale pink print, cut:
1 diamond
4 triangles

From the dark-pink tone on tone, cut:
4 rectangles, 1¼" x 10"
2 triangles

From the large-scale pink print, cut:
4 strips, 3½" x 42"

From the multicolored stripe, cut:
4 strips, 3½" x 42"

Alternate Colorway

This design works with all kinds of prints. Pick three coordinating prints that fit your decor, add a fabric for the background, and start sewing!

ASSEMBLING THE TABLE RUNNER

Sew with right sides together using a ¼" seam allowance.

1. From the backing fabric, make a piece approximately 15" x 55". Refer to "Baste the Backing and Batting Together" (page 68) to attach the batting to the wrong side of the backing rectangle using your favorite method.
2. Draw lines on the batting through the vertical and horizontal centers to mark the rectangle center. Center the small-scale pink-print diamond on the batting, right side up; pin it in place.

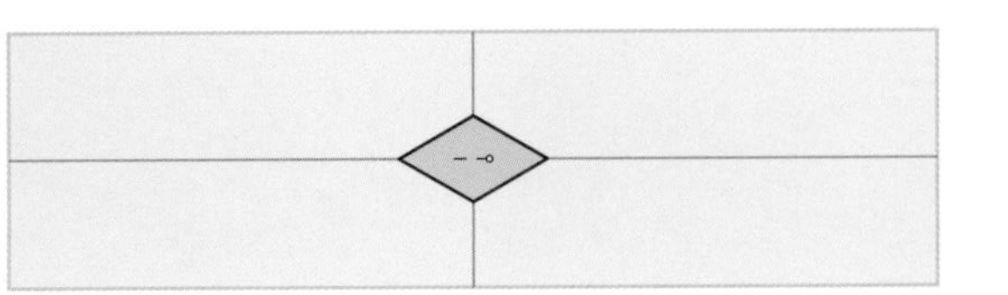

3. Center two dark-pink 1¼" x 10" rectangles on opposite sides of the diamond, aligning the raw edges; pin in place. Sew the rectangles in place through all the layers. Press the rectangles open. Trim the rectangle ends even with the diamond sides.

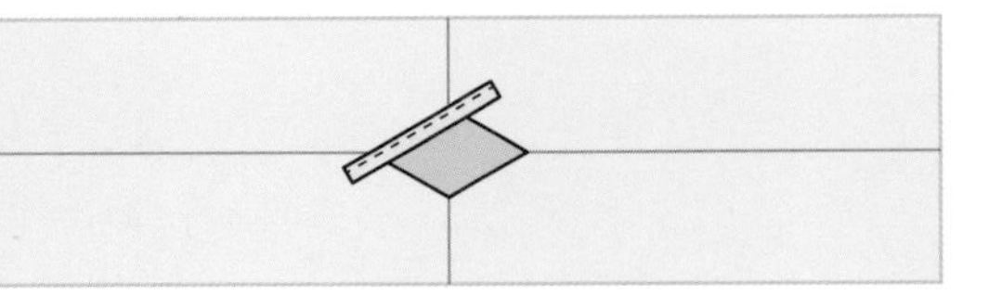

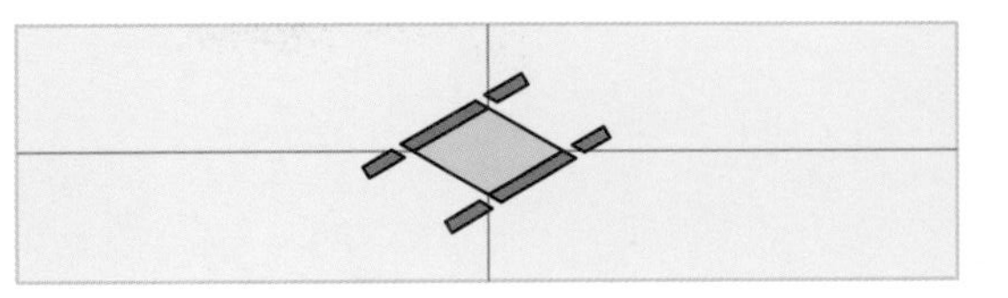

4. Center the remaining two dark-pink 1¼" x 10" rectangles on the remaining sides of the diamond; pin and then stitch in place. Press the rectangles open, and then trim the ends even with the previous dark-pink rectangles.

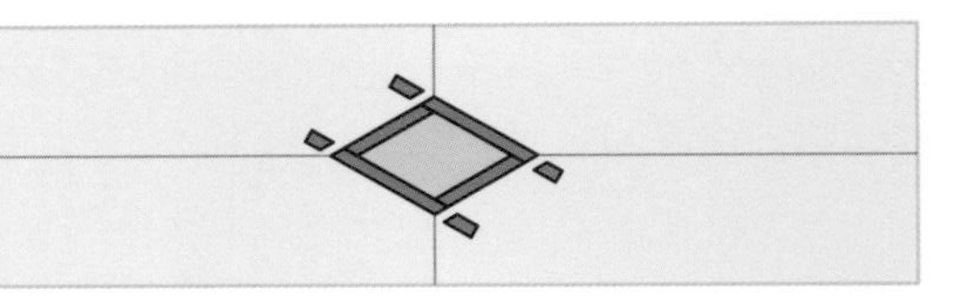

5. Center two white 3½" x 7½" rectangles on opposite sides of the diamond unit, aligning the raw edges; pin and then sew in place. Press the rectangles open.

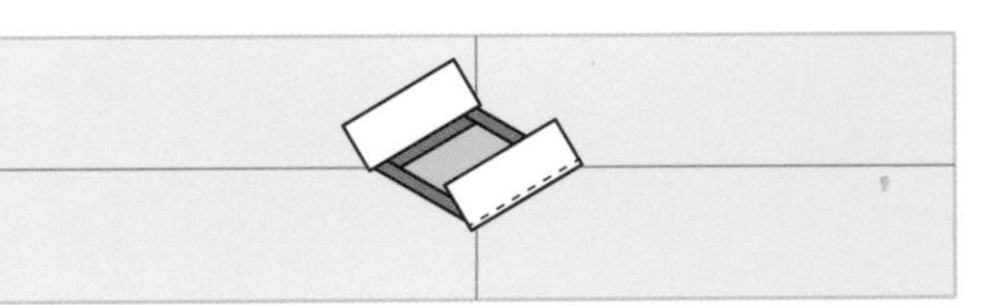

6. Repeat step 5 on the opposite sides of the diamond unit.

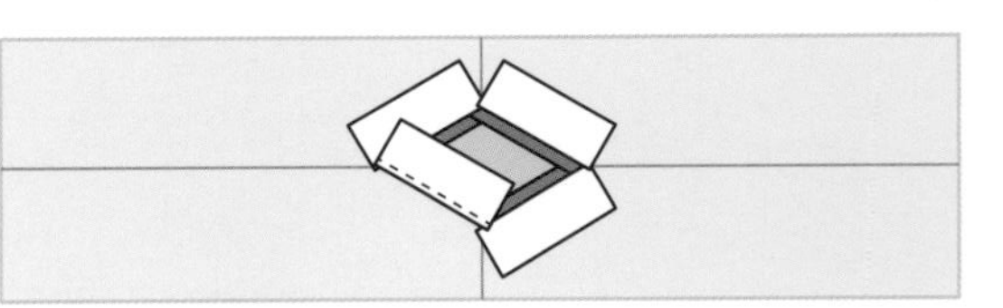

7. Lay a ruler on the pieced unit, aligning the ¼" line of the ruler with one point of the diamond. Use the marked line on the batting to make sure the ruler is parallel, and then mark a line that spans the pieced unit. Repeat on all of the remaining points of the diamond to mark

a rectangle. These will be the placement lines for the triangles.

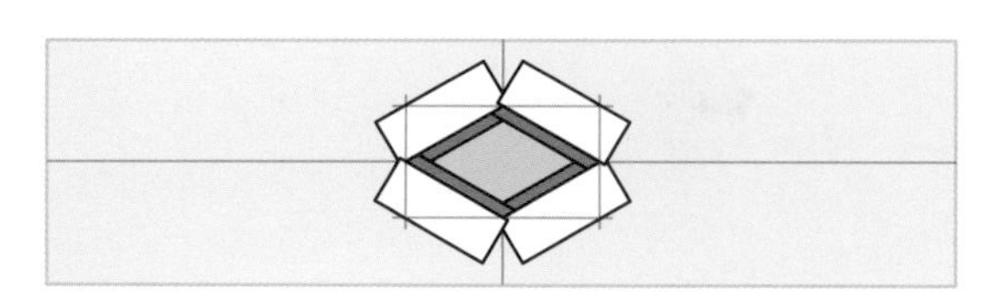

8. Refer to "Adding Triangles to a Straight Setting" (page 72) to fold each triangle in half and finger-press the fold to mark the center.

9. Center a small-scale pink-print triangle on each side of the diamond unit, matching the fold lines to the diamond points, and aligning the edge of each triangle with the marked vertical lines; pin and then stitch the triangles in place. Trim the white fabric that extends past the stitched side of each triangle even with the triangle. Press the triangles open.

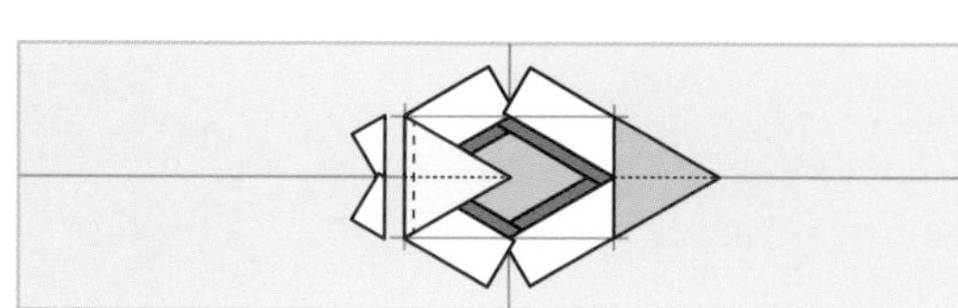

10. Center, pin, and then stitch white 3½" x 7½" rectangles to the raw edges of each triangle. Press the rectangles open.

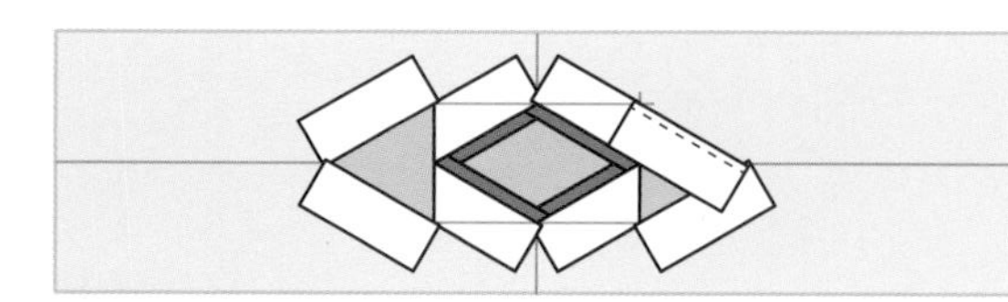

11. Lay your ruler along a drawn horizontal line, aligning the ¼" line of the ruler with the points of the triangles. Extend the drawn line through the pieced unit, making sure it's parallel to the horizontal center line. Repeat with the remaining horizontal line. In the same manner, extend the vertical lines, keeping them parallel to the vertical center line.

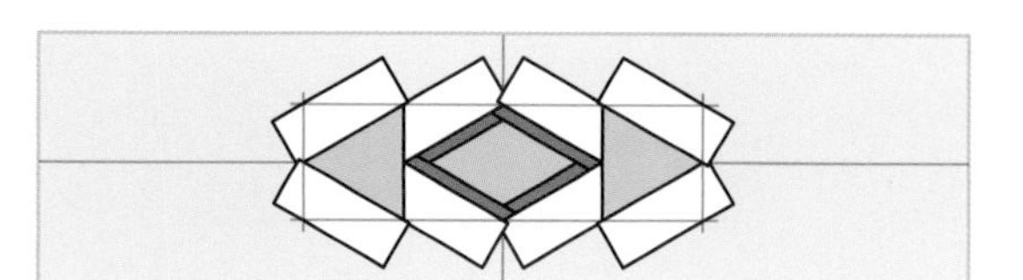

12. Repeat steps 9–11 two more times, using the dark-pink triangles and then the small-scale pink-print triangles and adding the white rectangles after each triangle has been stitched in place.

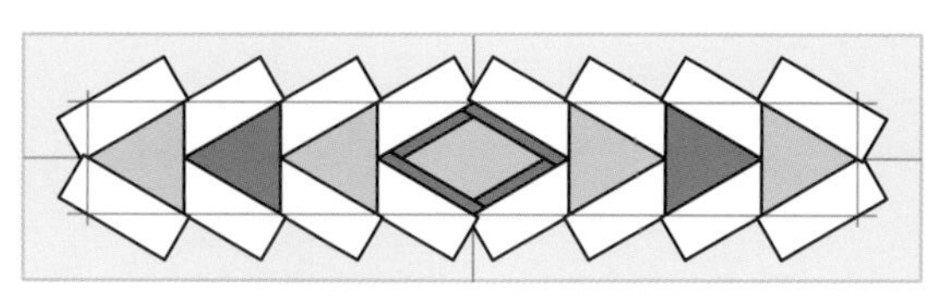

13. Join the large-scale pink-print 3½" x 42" strips end to end using diagonal seams to make one long strip. Press the seam allowances open. Lay the strip along the horizontal placement line and trim the ends even with the vertical placement lines. Pin and then stitch the strip in place. Trim the white rectangles even with the strip long edges. Press the border strip open. Repeat on the opposite horizontal line.

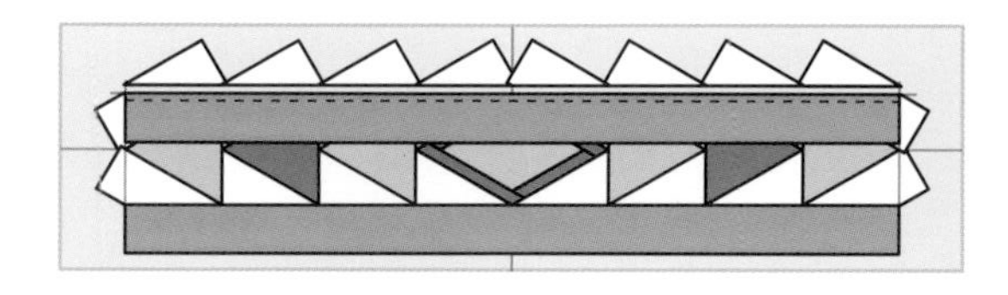

14. Using the remainder of the pieced strip, repeat step 13 to add borders to the short edges.

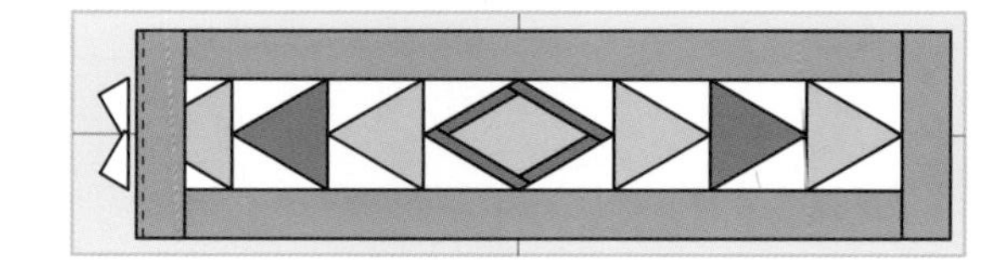

FINISHING

1. Trim the batting and backing even with the runner-top edges.

2. Refer to "Binding" (page 76) to join the multicolored 2½"-wide strips into one long strip and use it to bind the runner edges.

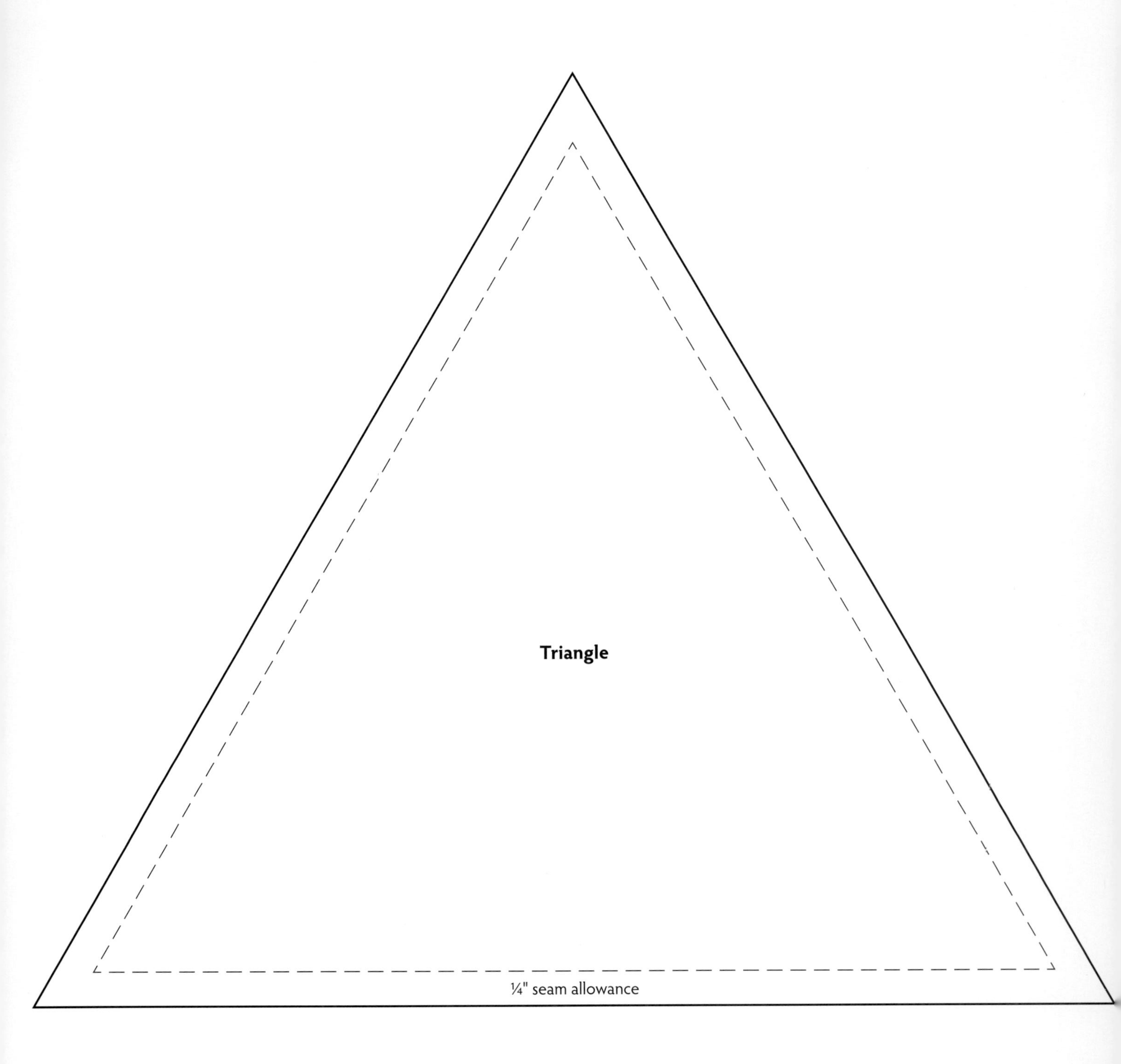
Triangle
¼" seam allowance

Diamond

¼" seam allowance

Stripalicious
TABLE RUNNER

FINISHED TABLE RUNNER: 10½" x 40½"

Alternate straight and diagonally placed strips to create this yummy table runner. Whether done in brights, pastels, prints, or solids, it's sure to be the focal point of any room.

MATERIALS

Yardage is based on 42"-wide fabric.

12 strips, 2" x 42", of assorted bright batiks for top
¼ yard of multicolored batik for binding
½ yard of fabric for backing
12" x 42" piece of batting

CUTTING

From the backing fabric, cut:
1 rectangle, 14" x 44"

From the multicolored batik, cut:
3 strips, 2½" x 42"

ASSEMBLING THE TABLE RUNNER

Refer to "Sewing by Numbers" on page 72 for general instructions about marking the batting and sewing the strips in place. Sew with right sides together using a ¼" seam allowance.

1. Refer to "Baste the Backing and Batting Together" (page 68) to attach the batting to the wrong side of the backing rectangle using your favorite method.
2. Draw two horizontal lines 10" apart on the batting. Mark a vertical line about 2" from the left edge of the batting. Draw four more vertical lines, each 10" apart. Then draw diagonal lines through each 10" square, alternating the directions as shown on page 32. Make sure the lines extend through the square about 1" to 2". Finally, draw a line ¼" to the left of the first

vertical line to use as the placement guide for the first strip. Number the triangles from 1 to 8 as shown. This will be the order in which you fill each section.

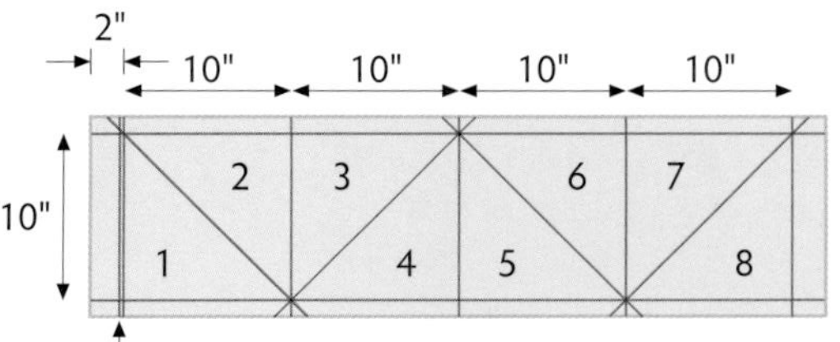

3. Select a 2" x 42" strip and lay it right side up on the batting, aligning the left raw edge of the strip with the placement line on the batting, and extending the top of the strip at least ¼" past the top horizontal line on the batting. Trim the strip so it extends past the bottom horizontal line at least ¼"; pin in place. Lay another strip to the right of the first strip so it extends past the diagonal line at least ¼". Trim the strip so it extends past the bottom horizontal line at least ¼". Flip the strip over onto the first strip and align the raw edges on the right edge of the first strip. Pin and then stitch the strip in place through all the layers. Press the strip open.

   Continue adding strips of different colors in this manner until about half of section 1 is filled. Align the ¼" line on your ruler with the original diagonal placement line and draw a new placement line across the newly added strips.

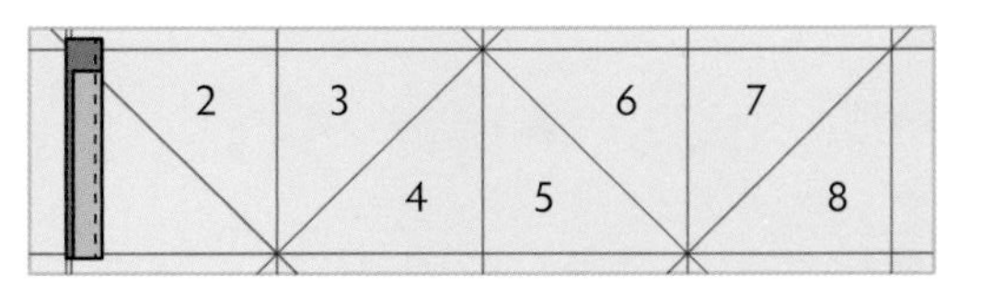

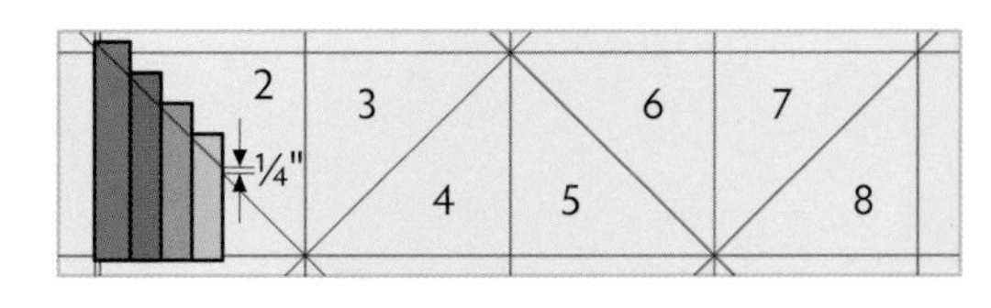

4. Continue adding strips in the same manner until section 1 is completely filled. Extend the diagonal placement line across the newly added strips, and draw a new placement line ¼" from the original horizontal line across the bottom of section 1.

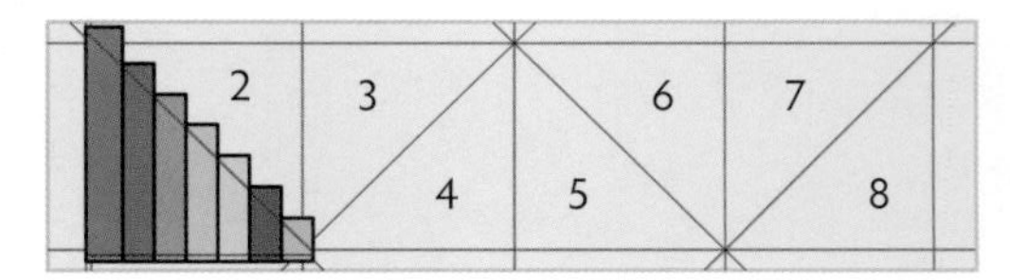

5. Place a strip diagonally on section 1, right side down, aligning the right edge of the strip with the diagonal placement line. Pin and then sew the strip in place along the right edge. Trim the ends of the strips in section 1 even with the newly added strip, if desired. Press the strip open.

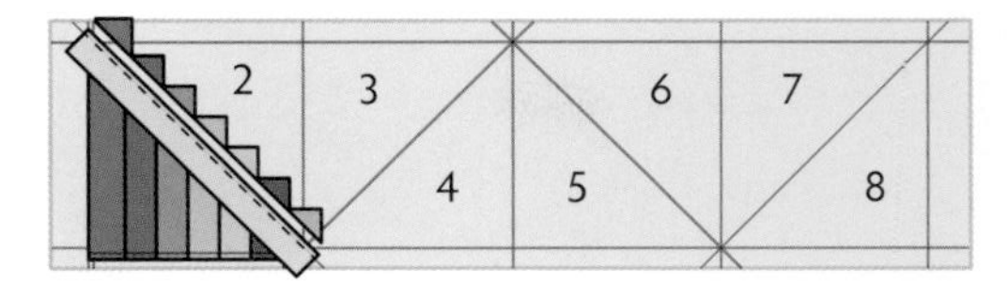

6. Fill in section 2 in the same manner as for section 1. When the area is completely filled, draw a horizontal line across the top of the filled square, ¼" from the original horizontal line, and another line ¼" from the vertical line between sections 2 and 3.

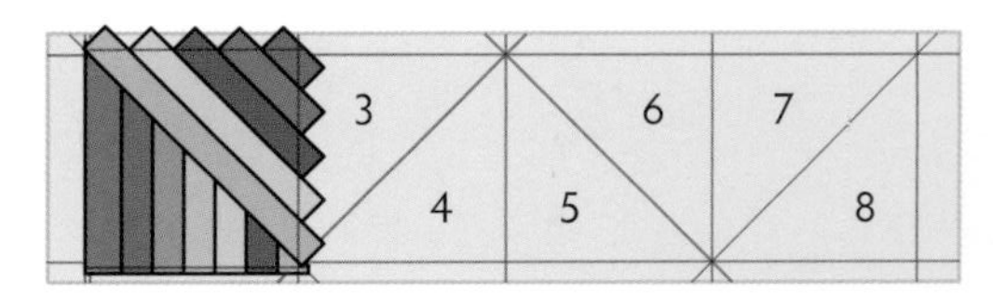

7. Repeat steps 3–6 to fill in each triangular area in numerical order until all eight areas are covered.

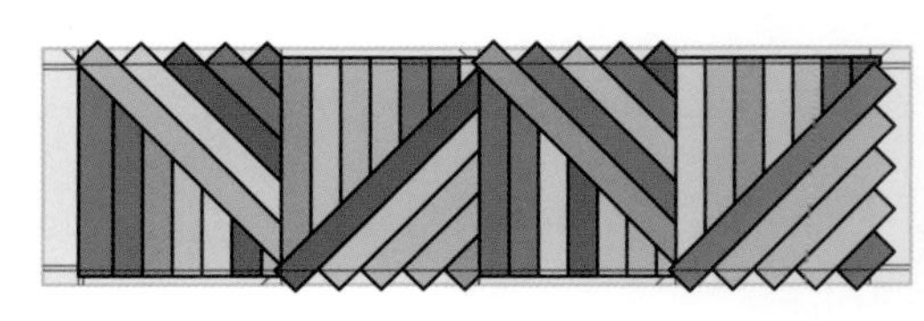

FINISHING

1. Trim along the drawn lines on top of the fabric through all the layers.

2. Refer to "Binding" (page 76) to join the 2½"-wide binding strips into one long strip and use it to bind the runner edges.

Spring Bouquet
WALL HANGING

FINISHED WALL HANGING: 32½" x 32½"

Fabric strips dance to and fro in this sweet wall hanging to create a quilt with lots of movement. Use a roll of precut strips from your favorite fabric collection to make it go even quicker, or cut coordinating strips from your stash.

MATERIALS

Yardage is based on 42"-wide fabric.

20 strips, 1½" x 42", of coordinating prints for top center and border corners
⅝ yard of coordinating solid for border
1 fat quarter (18" x 21") of green print for stem and leaf appliqués
Scraps of assorted pink prints for circle appliqués
⅓ yard of fabric for binding
1⅛ yards of fabric for backing
36" x 36" piece of batting
½ yard of 17"-wide paper-backed fusible web

CUTTING

Refer to "Adding Appliqués" (page 74) and use the patterns on page 39 to prepare appliqué shapes A–N.

From the backing fabric, cut:
1 square, 36" x 36"

From the coordinating solid, cut:
4 strips, 4½" x 24½"

From the green print, cut:
4 *each* using patterns A, B, and C
1 *each* using patterns H, K, and L
2 using pattern I
1 *each* using patterns I reversed and J

From the assorted pink scraps, cut a *total* of:
4 using pattern D
15 using pattern E
9 using pattern F
1 *each* using patterns G and N
7 using pattern M

From the binding fabric, cut:
4 strips, 2½" x 42"

ASSEMBLING THE WALL HANGING

Refer to "Sewing by Numbers" on page 72 for general instructions about marking the batting and sewing the strips in place. Sew with right sides together using a ¼" seam allowance.

1. Refer to "Baste the Backing and Batting Together" (page 68) to attach the batting to the wrong side of the backing square using your favorite method.

2. Draw a 16" square in the center of the batting, extending the lines at the corners as shown. Mark 4" out from the center square on each side and draw another square, again extending the lines at the corners. Mark the center of each side of the 16" square and draw diagonal lines from point to point as shown by the gray lines. Make sure to extend the lines 1" to 2". Draw diagonal lines across the point of each corner on both the 16" square and the 24" square by laying the 45° line on your ruler along the side of the square to get the correct angle. Finally, draw a vertical line through the center of the 16" square and another line ¼" to the right of the line to use as the placement guide for the first strip. Number the areas from 1 to 7 as shown. This will be the order in which you fill each area. Areas with the same number can be filled at the same time.

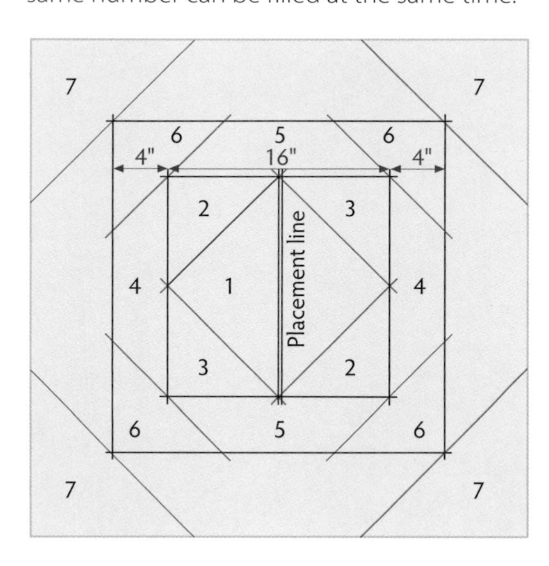

3. Select a 1½" x 42" strip and lay it right side up on the batting, aligning the right edge of the strip with the placement line on the batting, and extending the top of the strip at least ¼" past the top horizontal line of the 16" square. Trim the strip so it extends past the bottom horizontal line of the 16" square at least ¼". Select another strip and trim it to the same length as the first strip. Lay this strip on the first strip, right sides together with the raw edges aligned. Stitch the strips together along the right edge; press the strip open.

   Continue adding strips on both sides of these strips in the same manner, trimming the strips so they extend beyond the diagonal lines. When area 1 is about halfway complete, align the ¼" line of your ruler with each of the original diagonal lines and draw new placement lines for areas 2 and 3 across the strips.

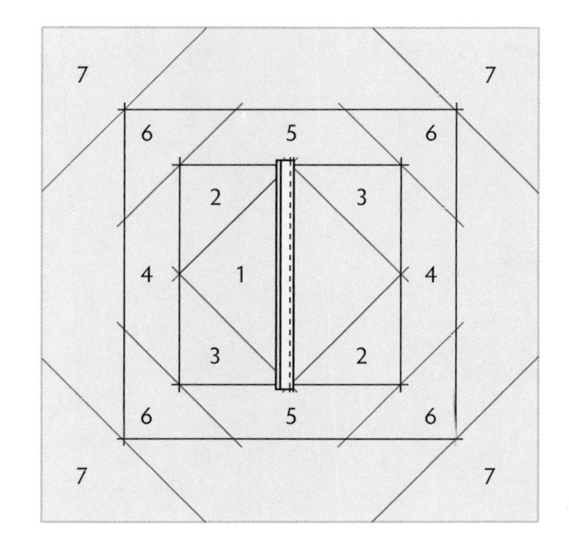

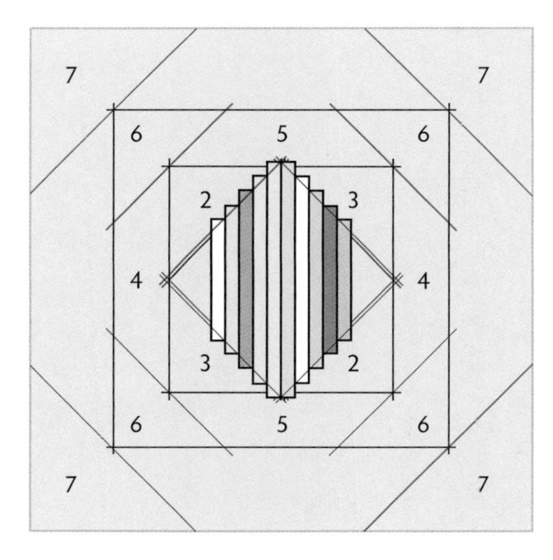

4. Continue adding strips in the same manner until area 1 is completely filled. Extend the placement line across the newly added strips.

5. Lay a strip diagonally along the placement line of one area 2, right sides together. Trim the strip so it extends at least ¼" past the top and side edges of the 16" square; pin and then stitch in place. Trim the ends of the strips in area 1 even with the strip edges, if desired. Repeat for the remaining area 2.

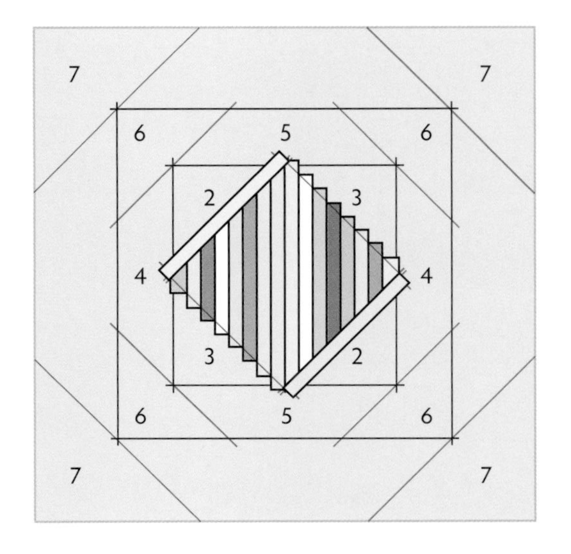

6. Continue adding strips in the same manner to each area 2 until they are completely filled. Draw new placement lines ¼" from the original top and side lines. Then fill each area 3 in the same manner, and extend the placement line across the newly added strips.

7. Fill each area 4 and then each area 5 as before. Draw the diagonal placement lines for each area 6.

8. Fill in each area 6 as before, and draw the placement lines for the areas with no numbers, ¼" outside of the 24" square.

9. Stitch the coordinating-solid 4½" x 24½" strips to the sides of the quilt top, aligning the raw edge of each strip with the placement line. Press the strips open. Repeat with the remaining solid 4½" x 24½" strips to add the top and bottom borders to the quilt top. Draw the diagonal placement lines for each area 7.

10. Fill in each area 7 as before, making sure the strips are long enough to extend past each side of the border strips.

FINISHING

1. Trim the layers even with the edges of the border strips.
2. Refer to "Adding Appliqués" (page 74) and the placement diagram below to fuse the appliqué shapes to the center and border strips. Stitch each appliqué in place.
3. Refer to "Binding" (page 76) to join the 2½"-wide binding strips into one long strip and use it to bind the wall-hanging edges.

Appliqué placement

B
C
D
E
F
I
Ir
J
G
A
H
K
L
M
N

Patterns are reversed for fusible appliqué.

Flipped Chevrons
TABLE RUNNER

FINISHED TABLE RUNNER: 16½" x 42½"

Rows of prairie points give dimension and pizzazz to this modern table runner. Use fabrics that gradate from light to dark to make each row stand out.

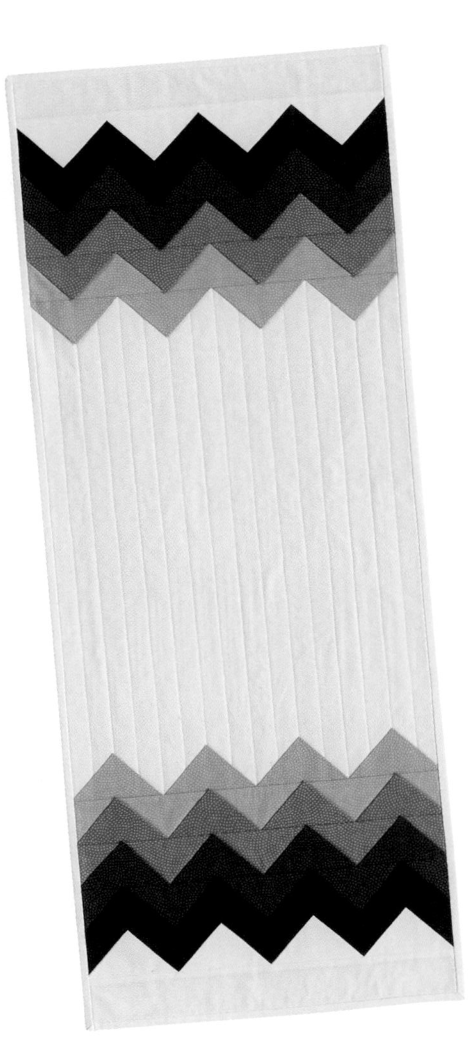

MATERIALS

Yardage is based on 42"-wide fabric.

¾ yard of white solid for background and binding
¼ yard *each* of light-blue, medium-blue, medium-dark-blue, and dark-blue solid for chevrons
1⅜ yards of fabric for backing
19" x 45" piece of batting

CUTTING

From the backing fabric, cut:
1 rectangle, 19" x 45"

From the white solid, cut:
1 strip, 16½" x 42"; crosscut into:
 1 rectangle, 16½" x 22½"
 2 rectangles, 2½" x 16½"
3 strips, 2½" x 42"
8 squares, 4½" x 4½"

From *each* of the blue solids, cut:
1 strip, 2½" x 42"; crosscut into 2 rectangles, 2½" x 16½" (8 total)
1 strip, 4½" x 42"; crosscut into 8 squares, 4½" x 4½" (32 total)

ASSEMBLING THE TABLE RUNNER

Sew with right sides together using a ¼" seam allowance.

1. Refer to "Baste the Backing and Batting Together" (page 68) to attach the batting to the wrong side of the backing rectangle using your favorite method.
2. With the batting side out, fold the backing/batting sandwich in half vertically and horizontally to find the center. Mark the center point on the batting using a water-soluble pen. Fold the white 16½" x 22½" rectangle in half vertically and horizontally and finger-press the folds to mark the center. With the centers aligned, lay the white rectangle on the batting, right side up. Pin it in place, and then quilt it however you want. I quilted parallel lines every 1", beginning 1½" from the long edges, using my walking foot.

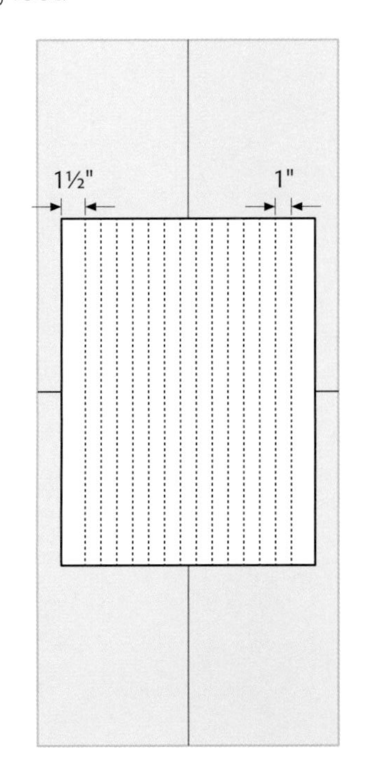

3. Refer to "Playing with Prairie Points" (page 74) to fold and press all of the white and blue 4½" squares into prairie points (40 total).
4. With the raw edges aligned, position four light-blue prairie points on each end of the quilted rectangle, overlapping them about ¼" so they fit across the edge. Lay a light-blue 2½" x 16½" rectangle over each row of triangles, aligning the strip raw edges with the triangle raw edges; pin and then stitch in place through all the layers. Press the rectangles open, leaving the prairie points pointing toward the center of the table runner.

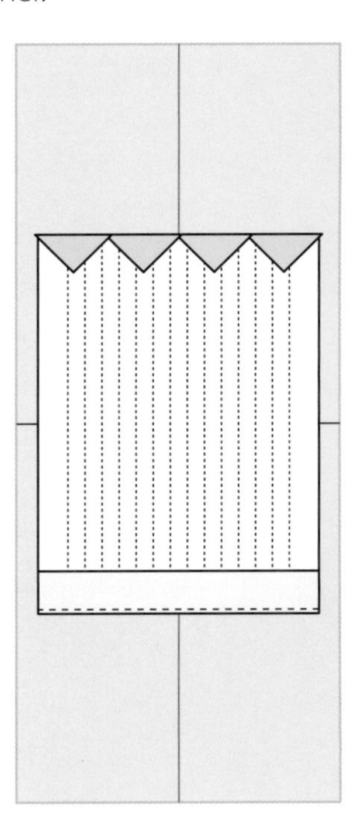

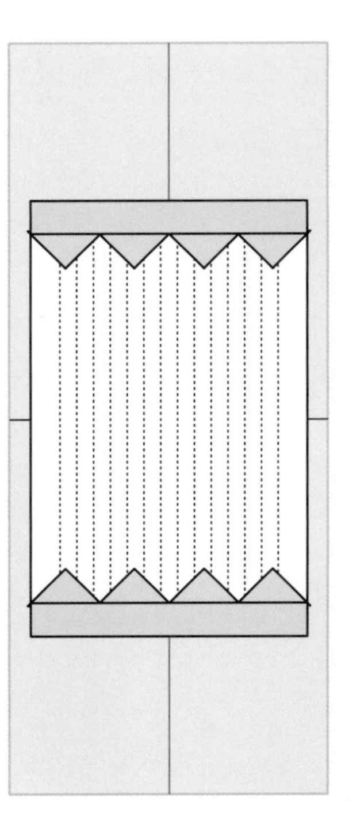

5. Repeat step 4 with the medium-blue prairie points and rectangles, followed by the medium-dark-blue prairie points and rectangles, the dark-blue prairie points and rectangles, and finally the white prairie points and rectangles.

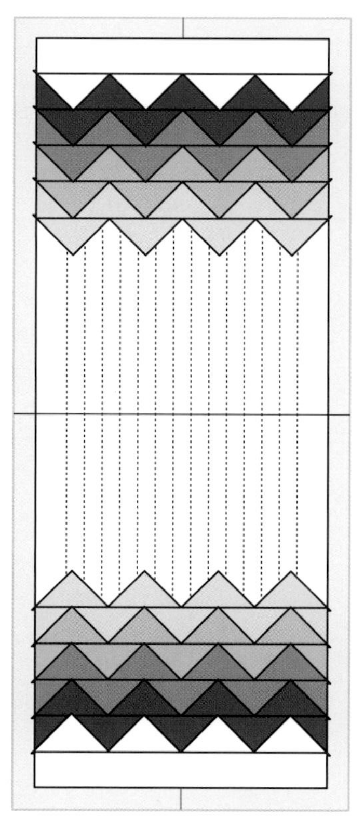

FINISHING

1. Trim the batting and backing even with the runner-top edges.
2. Refer to "Binding" (page 76) to join the white 2½"-wide strips into one long strip and use it to bind the runner edges.

Alternate Colorway

Flipped Chevrons Table Runner in alternate colorway. You don't have to stay with a monochromatic color scheme. Any combination of colors that gradate from light to dark will look great!

Lucky Charms
TOPPER

FINISHED TOPPER: 9" x 27"

Lay this little topper on a side table, drape it across the back of a chair, or hang it on a skinny wall. No matter where you place it, this little quilt will provide just the right accent.

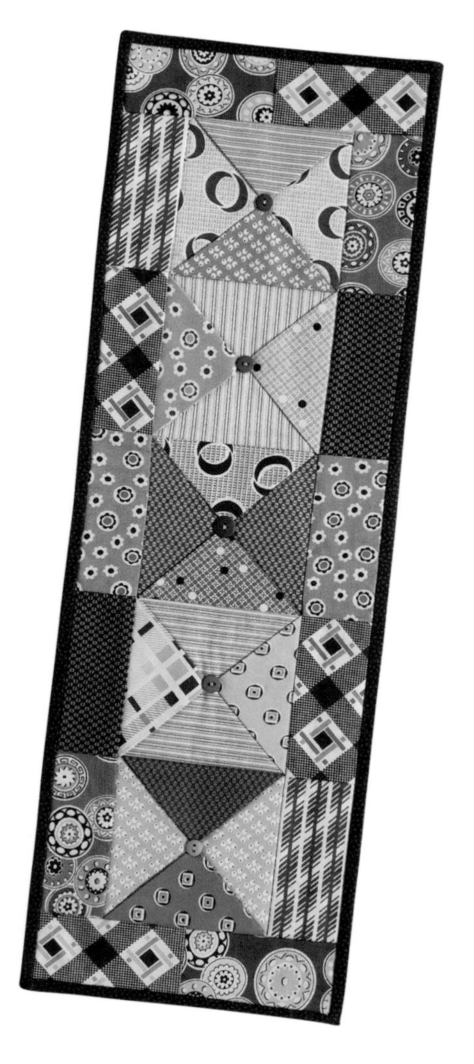

MATERIALS

Yardage is based on 42"-wide fabric.

22 charm squares (5" x 5") of assorted prints for background, prairie points, and border
¼ yard of fabric for binding
⅜ yard of fabric for backing
11" x 29" piece of batting
5 assorted ⅜"- to ½"-diameter buttons

Front and Back Charm

If you have a charm pack with at least 34 squares, choose 22 of them for the front and piece the remaining 12 together for a charming backing.

CUTTING

From the backing fabric, cut:
1 rectangle, 11" x 29"

From the binding fabric, cut:
2 strips, 2½" x 42"

ASSEMBLING THE TOPPER

Sew with right sides together using a ¼" seam allowance.

1. Refer to "Baste the Backing and Batting Together" (page 68) to attach the batting rectangle to the wrong side of the backing rectangle using your favorite method.
2. Draw lines on the batting through the vertical and horizontal centers to mark the center of the batting.
3. Set aside seven charm squares to use for the border. Set aside another five charm squares for the background. Refer to "Playing with Prairie Points" (page 74) to fold and press the remaining 10 charm squares into prairie points.
4. Center a background charm square on the batting, right side up. Lay two prairie points on top of the square, aligning the raw edges with the left and right sides of the square; pin in place.

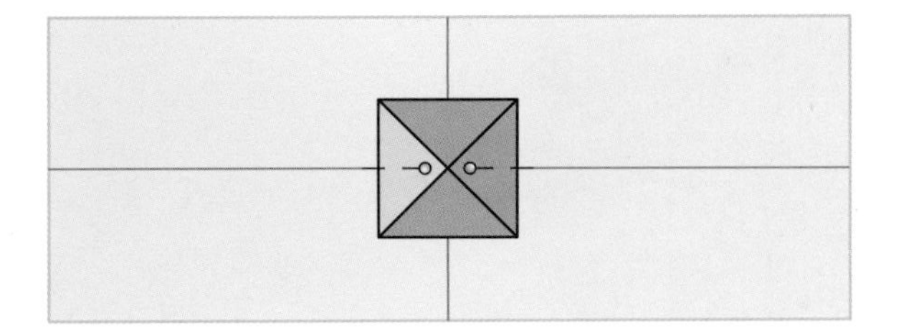

5. Pin the remaining prairie points to opposite edges of the remaining background squares as shown, aligning the raw edges.

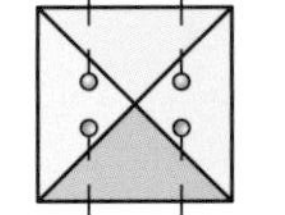

6. With the prairie points in opposite positions, lay a prepared unit from step 5 over the unit on the batting. Sew along the left edge of the units through all the layers; press the top unit open. Do not remove the pins holding the prairie points yet.

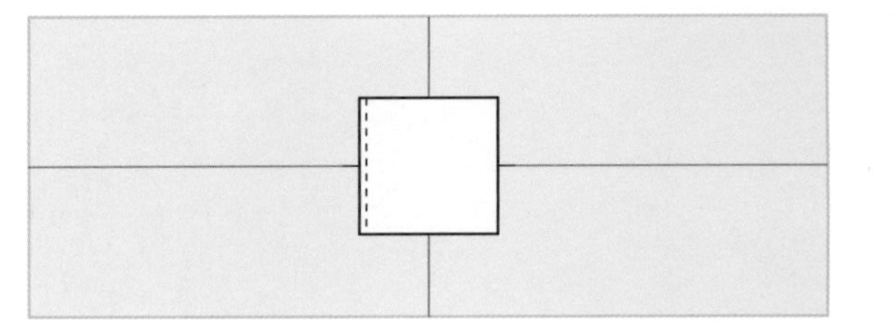

7. Repeat step 6, sewing a prepared unit to the opposite side of the center unit.

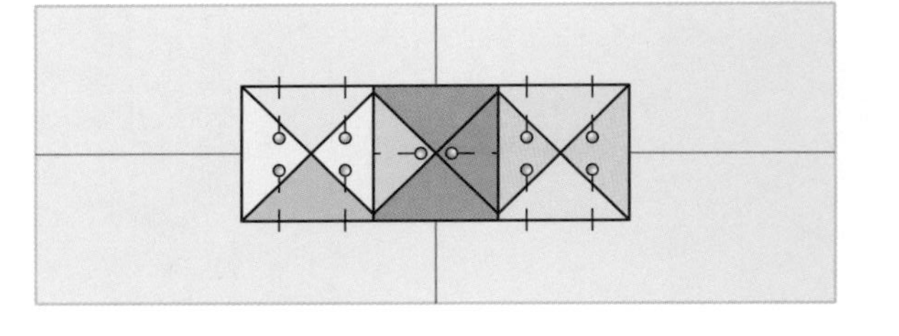

8. Add the remaining two prepared units from step 5 to the stitched unit in the same manner, rotating the prairie points a quarter turn so they are oriented the same as the center unit.

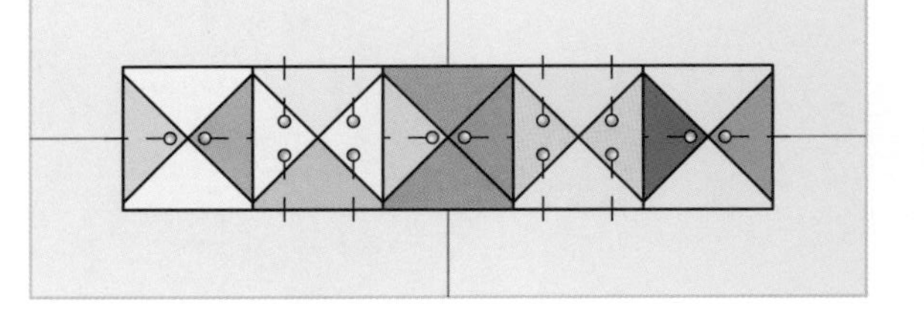

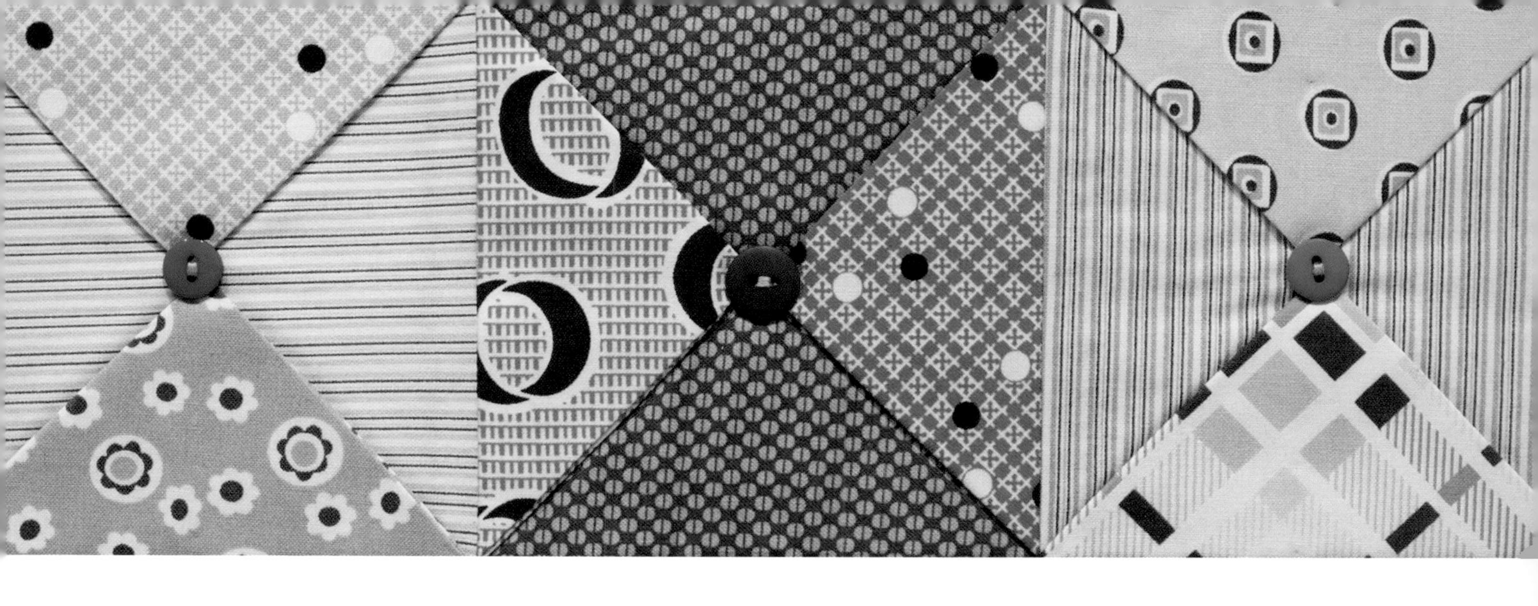

9. Sew together side by side five of the charm squares you set aside for the border. Repeat with the remaining two border squares. Press the seam allowances open. Cut each of the joined units in half lengthwise to make the border strips.

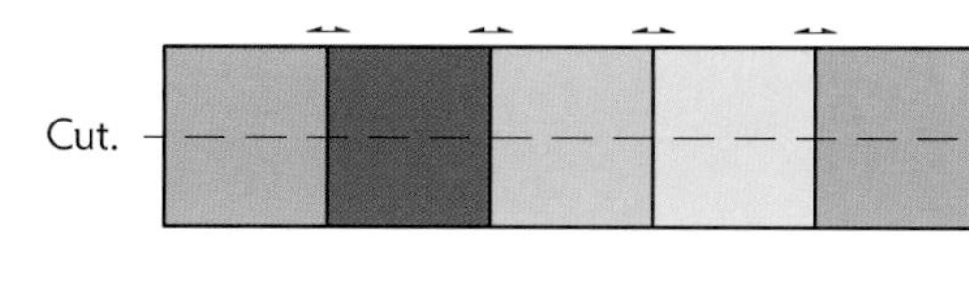

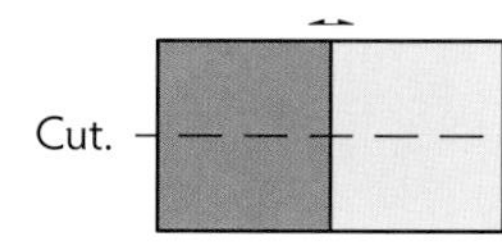

10. Join the long border strips to the long edges of the pieced center unit. Press the strips open.

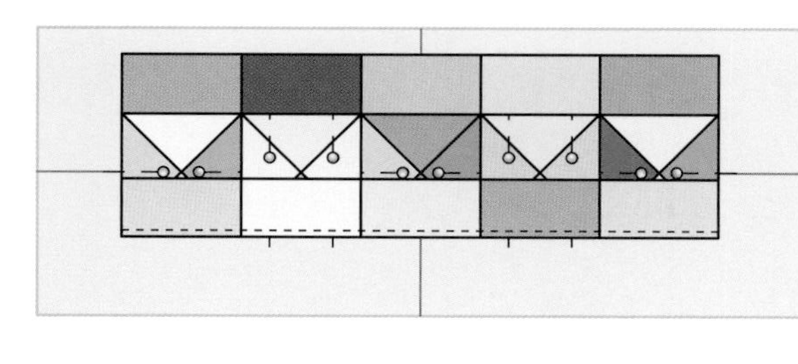

11. Add the short border strips to the short edges of the pieced center. Press the strips open.

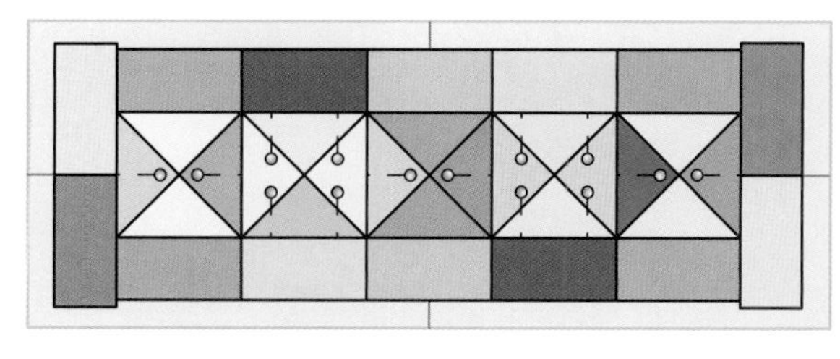

12. Sew a button through the center of each square, catching the prairie-point tips to secure them. If you don't want to use buttons, you can hand or machine tack the points in place, or use a decorative machine stitch to secure them. Remove the pins.

FINISHING

1. Trim the batting and backing even with the topper edges.
2. Refer to "Binding" (page 76) to join the 2½"-wide binding strips into one long strip and use it to bind the topper edges.

Gummy Candy
TABLE RUNNER

FINISHED TABLE RUNNER: 12½" x 51½"

Enjoy the sweetness of gumdrops without the added calories with this fun table runner.

MATERIALS

Yardage is based on 42"-wide fabric.

⅞ yard of white solid for background and binding
8½" x 8½" square *each* of 6 assorted bright solids for gumdrops
1 yard of fabric for backing
15" x 54" piece of batting

CUTTING

From the white solid, cut:
1 strip, 3" x 42"; crosscut into 12 squares, 3" x 3"
9 strips, 2½" x 42"; crosscut *2 of the strips* into 7 rectangles, 2½" x 9½"

ASSEMBLING THE TABLE RUNNER

Sew with right sides together using a ¼" seam allowance.

1. Using a pen or a pencil, measure 2" in from the left side of a bright-colored 8½" square and make a mark along the upper edge. Repeat on the right side of the square. Using a rotary cutter and ruler, cut from the bottom-left corner to the top-left mark and from the bottom-right corner to the top-right mark. Repeat with the remaining bright-colored squares.

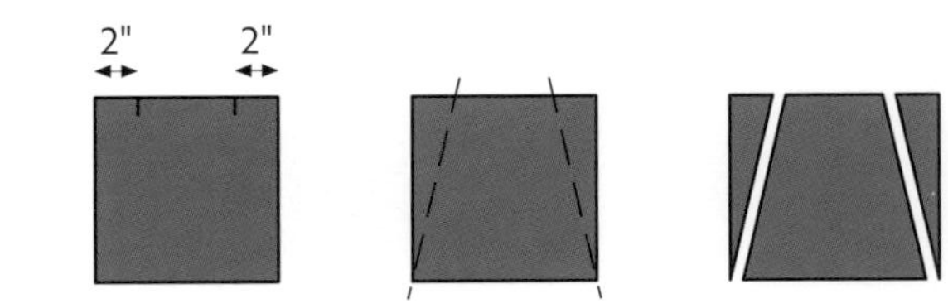

2. Press each white 3" square in half diagonally, wrong sides together. Place a triangle on each top corner of a wedge from step 1 as shown, aligning the bottom corner and the top edge of each triangle with the wedge; pin in place. Flip the wedge over and trim the excess triangle fabric so it follows the shape of the wedge. Prepare the remaining wedges in the same manner.

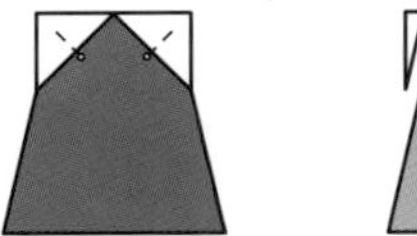
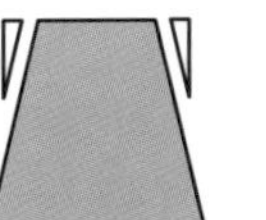

3. From the backing fabric, make a piece approximately 15" x 54". Refer to "Baste the Backing and Batting Together" (page 68) to attach the batting to the wrong side of the pieced backing rectangle using your favorite method. Draw a line on the batting through the vertical center. Draw two horizontal lines, 8½" apart, along the length of the batting. Place the first wedge on the batting, right side up, so that the bottom-left corner of the wedge touches the center line and the top and bottom edges of the wedge are aligned with the horizontal drawn lines; pin in place.

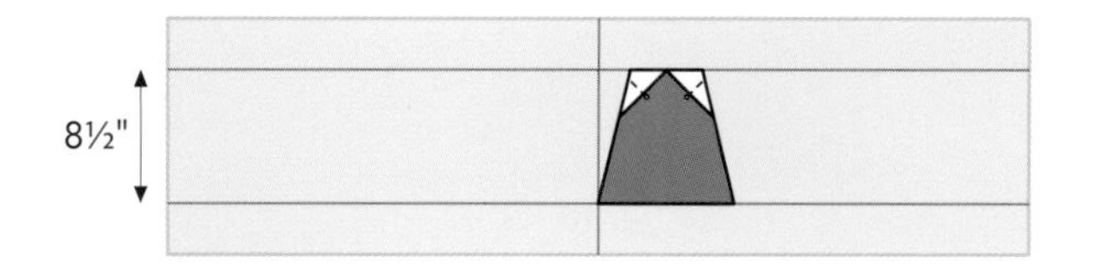

4. Center a white 2½" x 9½" rectangle on each side of the wedge, aligning the raw edges; pin in place. Sew the rectangles in place through all the layers. Press the rectangles open.

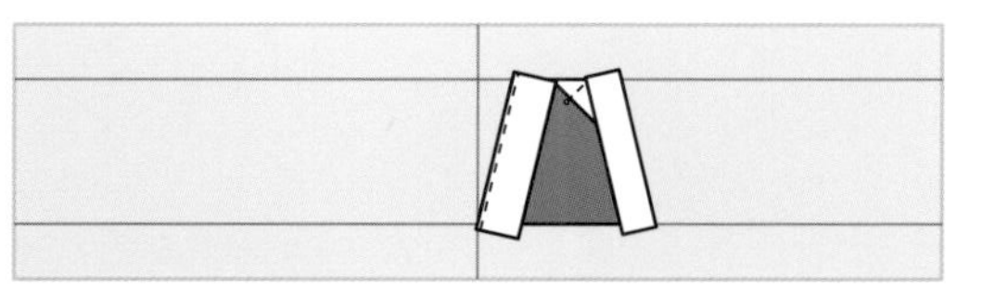

5. Sew a prepared wedge unit on each side of the first wedge, rotating the units as shown; press the wedge units open.

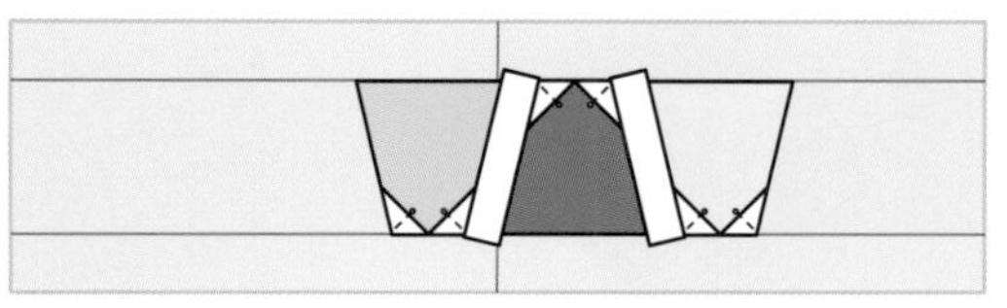

6. Repeat step 4 to add white rectangles to the sides of the wedge units attached in step 5. Press the rectangles open.

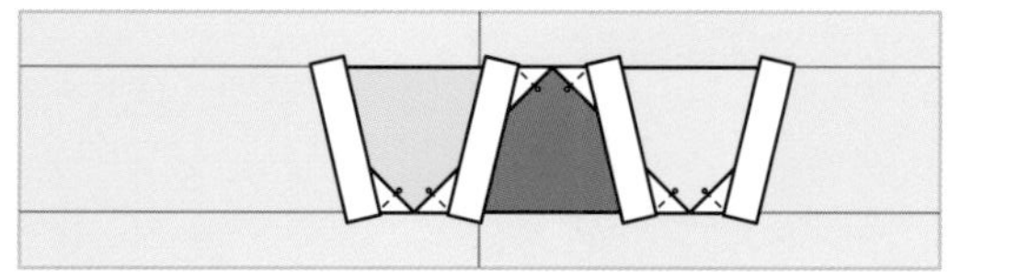

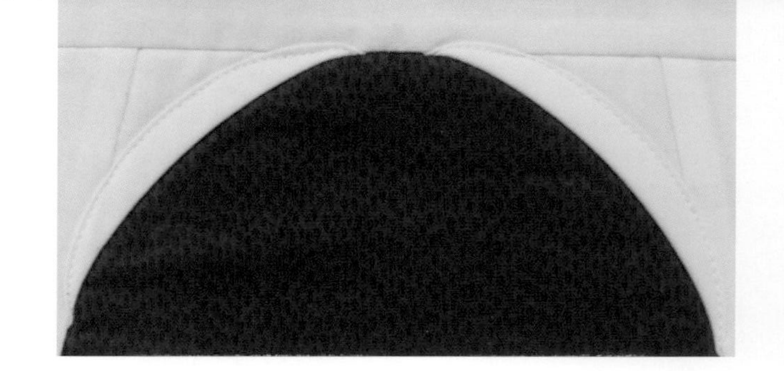

7. Continue alternatingly adding wedge units and rectangles to the backing/batting sandwich in this manner, rotating the wedge units as shown.

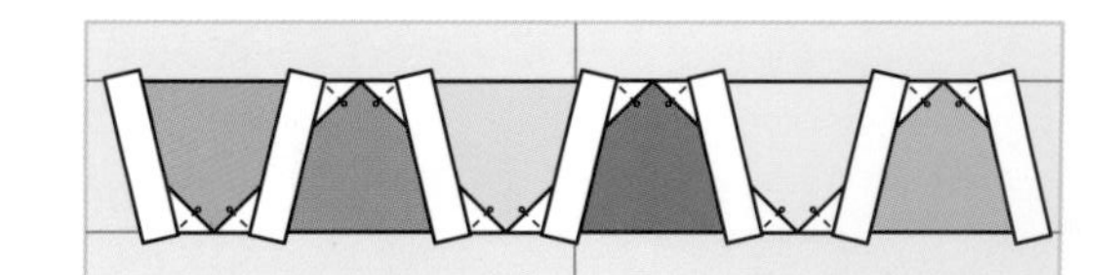

8. Sew three white 2½" x 42" strips together end to end using diagonal seams to make one long strip. Lay the pieced strip on the pieced unit, right sides together, aligning the long raw edge with the top horizontal placement line and the raw edges of the wedges. Trim the strip slightly longer on each end than the pieced unit. Sew the strip in place. Trim the ends of the white rectangles even with the wedges. Press the strip open. Using the remainder of the pieced strip, repeat on the opposite horizontal edge.

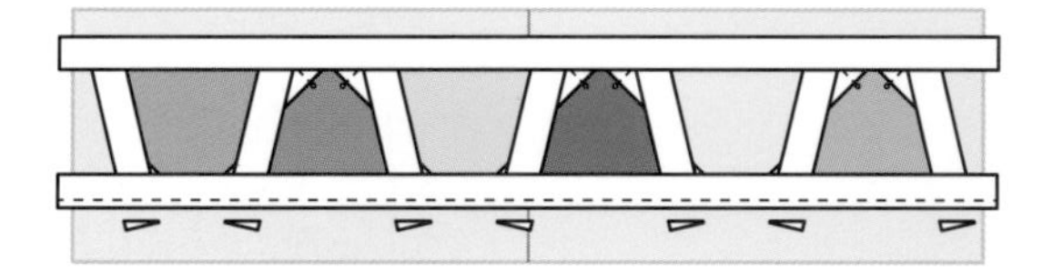

FINISHING

1. Trim the border strip ends even with the end rectangles through all the layers. Trim the batting and backing across the top and bottom edges even with the border strips.
2. Remove the pins from the white triangles. Refer to "Creating the Illusion of Curves" (page 75) to turn back the folded edge of each triangle to create a curve and edgestitch it in place.
3. Refer to "Binding" (page 76) to join the remaining four white 2½"-wide strips into one long strip and use it to bind the runner edges.

Petal Play
TOPPER

FINISHED TOPPER: 23½" x 23½"

Curves have never been so fun or quick to create as they are when using the quilt-as-you-go method. Watch each petal bloom as you simply turn back the edges of the background pieces and expose the colorful fabrics underneath.

MATERIALS

Yardage is based on 42"-wide fabric.

1⅛ yards of gray solid for background, border, and binding
21 charm squares (5" x 5") or scraps of assorted prints for petals and sashing squares
⅞ yard of fabric for backing
27" x 27" piece of batting

CUTTING

From the assorted prints, cut a *total* of:
16 squares, 4½" x 4½"
5 squares, 1½" x 1½"

From the gray solid, cut:
5 strips, 4½" x 42"; crosscut into:
32 squares, 4½" x 4½"
16 rectangles, 1½" x 4½"
1 strip, 1½" x 42"; crosscut into 4 rectangles, 1½" x 9½"
5 strips, 2½" x 42"

From the backing fabric, cut:
1 square, 27" x 27"

ASSEMBLING THE TOPPER

Sew with right sides together using a ¼" seam allowance.

1. Press each gray 4½" square in half diagonally, wrong sides together, to make a folded triangle. With the raw edges aligned, pin two folded triangles to the right side of an assorted-print 4½" square, butting the triangle folds at the center of the square. Pin the folded triangles in place. Repeat for the remaining assorted-print 4½" squares.

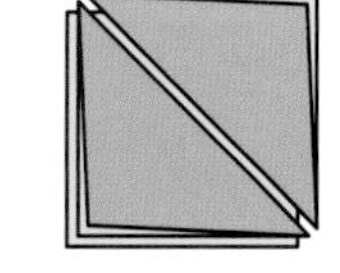

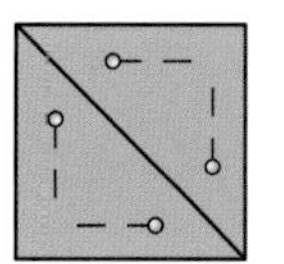

Make 16.

2. Sew a gray 1½" x 4½" rectangle between two units from step 1 as shown to make unit A. Make sure the triangle folds are oriented exactly as shown. Repeat to make a total of four A units. Press the seam allowances toward the rectangles.

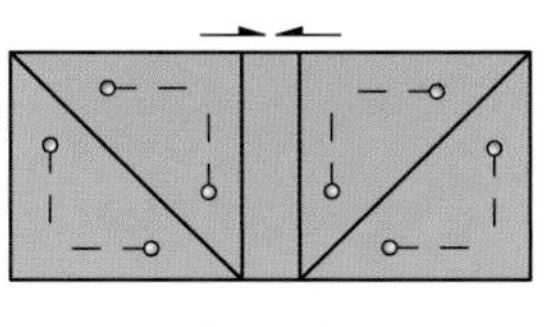

Unit A.
Make 4.

3. Alternately sew four units from step 1 and three gray 1½" x 4½" rectangles together as shown to make unit B. Again, make sure the triangle folds are oriented on the diagonals exactly as shown. Repeat to make a total of two B units. Press the seam allowances toward the rectangles.

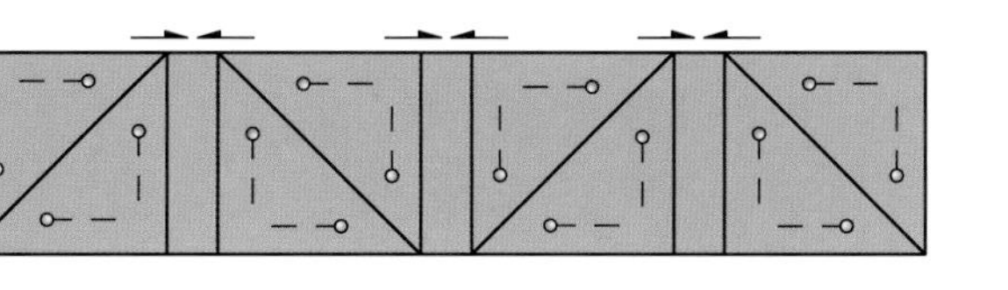

Unit B.
Make 2.

4. Sew a gray 1½" x 9½" rectangle between two assorted-print 1½" squares. Press the seam allowances toward the rectangles. Add a gray 1½" x 4½" rectangle to each end of the pieced strip. Press the seam allowances toward the rectangles. Repeat to make a total of two units.

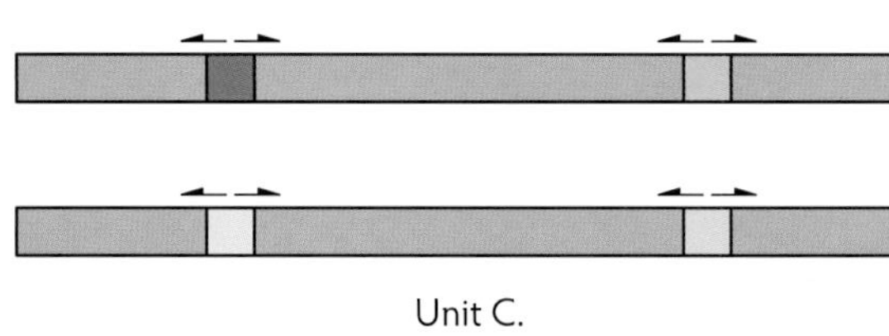

Unit C.
Make 2.

5. Refer to "Baste the Backing and Batting Together" (page 68) to attach the batting to the wrong side of the backing 27" square using your favorite method.

6. Draw lines on the batting through the vertical and horizontal centers to mark the square center. Center an assorted-print 1½" square on the batting, right side up. Pin a gray 1½" x 4½" rectangle to the square, right sides together, aligning the raw edges on the right edge of the square. Sew the pieces together through all the layers. Press the rectangle open.

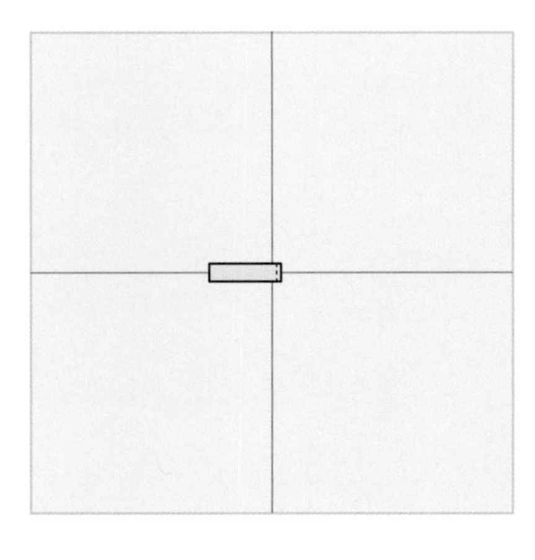

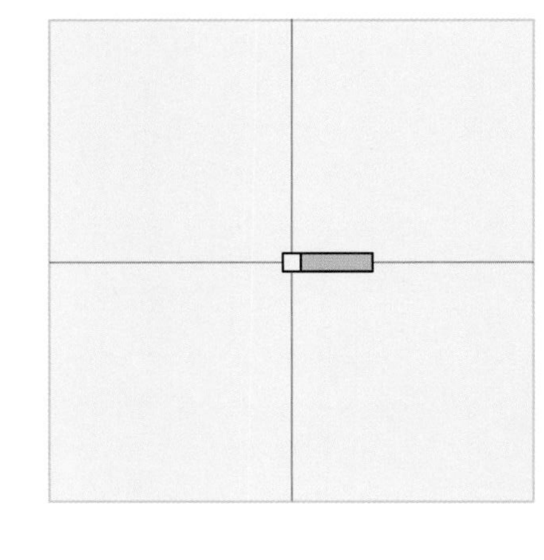

7. Pin a gray 1½" x 4½" rectangle to the left edge of the center square, and stitch it in place. Press the rectangle open.

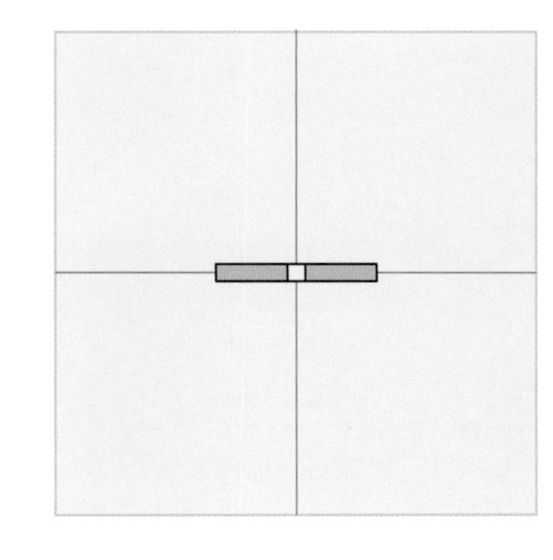

8. Pin and then sew an A unit to the top edge of the unit from step 7, making sure the unit is oriented correctly. Press the unit open. Do not remove the pins holding the triangles yet. Repeat to sew an A unit to the bottom edge of the unit from step 7, making sure the unit is oriented correctly. Press the unit open.

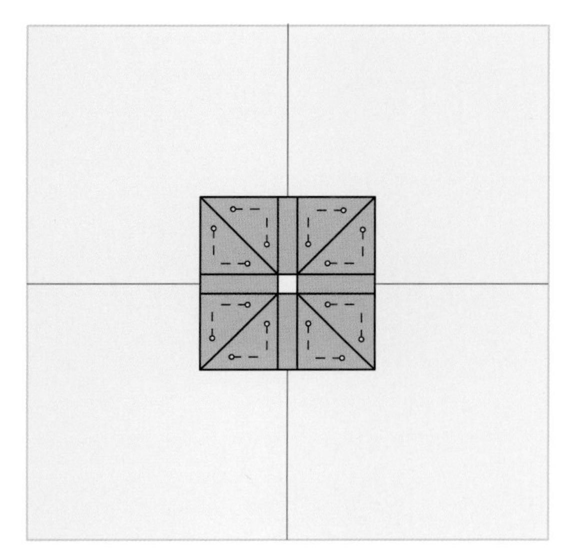

9. Sew gray 1½" x 9½" rectangles to the top and bottom edges of the unit from step 8. Press the rectangles open.

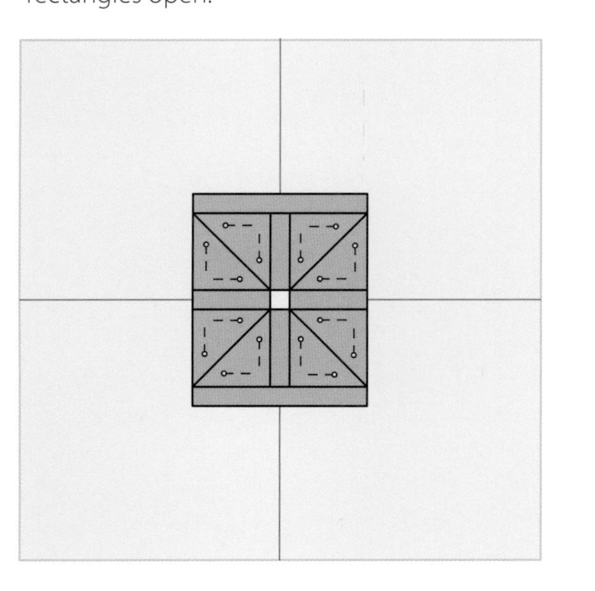

10. Repeat step 8 to sew the remaining A units to the top and bottom edges of the unit from step 9, making sure the units are oriented exactly as shown. Press the units open.

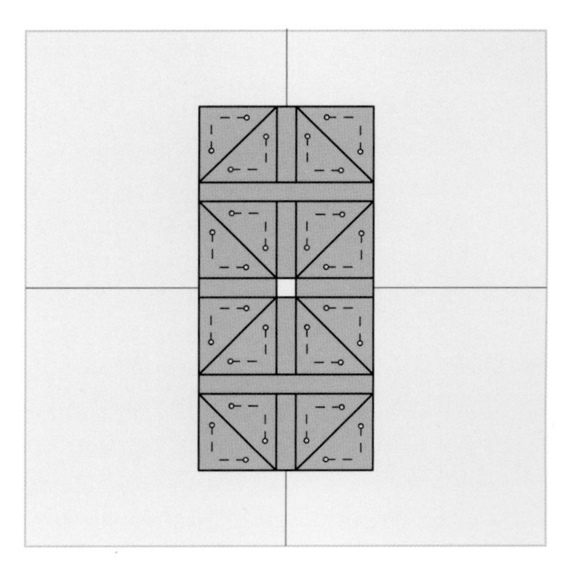

11. Sew the C units to the sides of the unit from step 10. Press the units open.

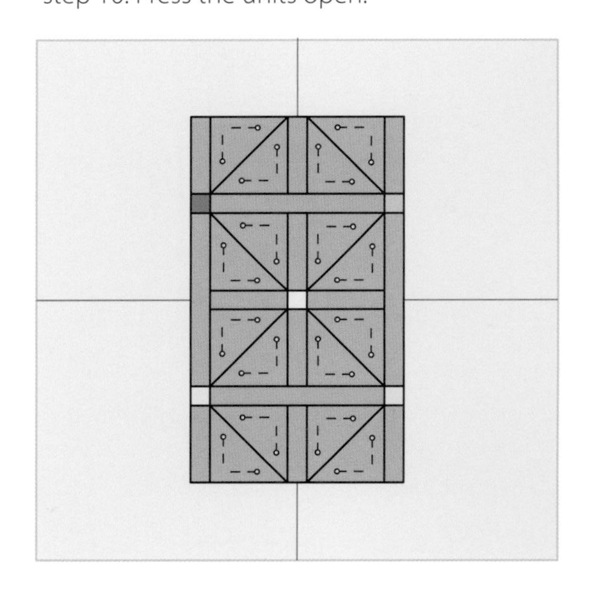

12. Sew the B units to the sides of the unit from step 11, making sure the units are oriented exactly as shown. Press the units open.

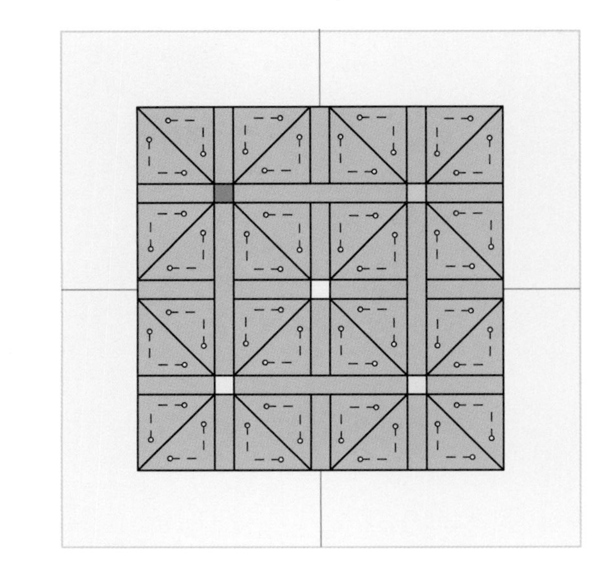

13. Sew the gray 2½" x 42" strips together end to end using diagonal seams to make one long strip. Lay the long strip along the top edge of the unit, right sides together, aligning the raw edges. Trim the strip to the same length as the top edge. Pin and then stitch the strip in place. Press the strip open. Repeat on the bottom edge and then both sides of the unit. Set aside the remainder of the pieced strip for the binding.

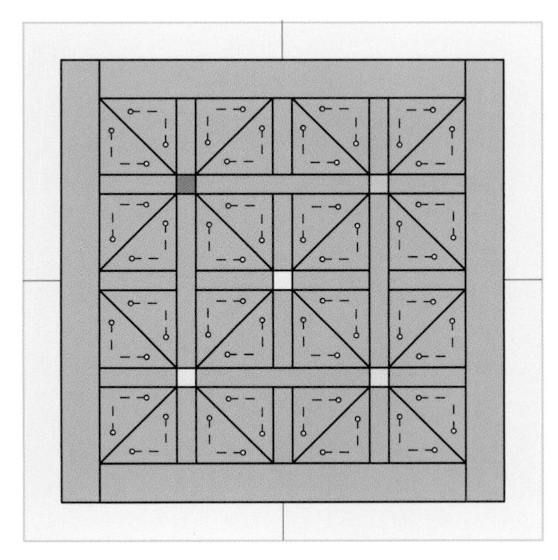

FINISHING

1. Trim the batting and backing even with the topper edges.
2. Remove the pins from all of the folded triangles. Refer to "Creating the Illusion of Curves" (page 75) to turn back the folded edge of each triangle to create a curve and edgestitch it in place. Because the edge you're turning is bias, it will automatically curve into place.

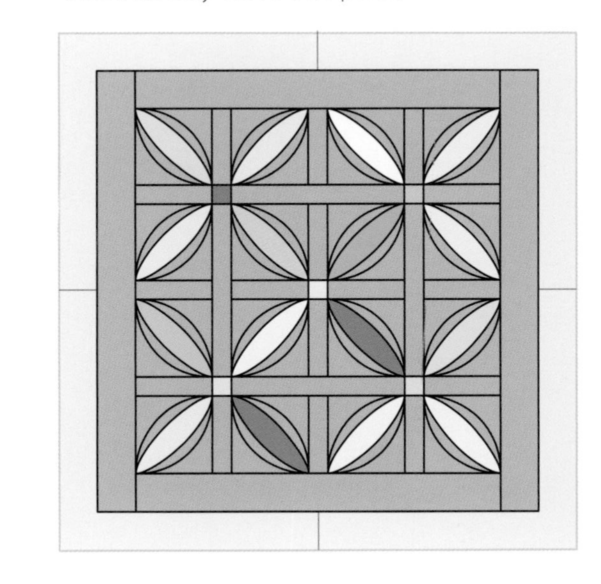

3. Refer to "Binding" (page 76) to use the remainder of the pieced gray strip to bind the topper edges.

In the Round
PLACE MATS

FINISHED PLACE MATS: 16" diameter

Enhance your dining experience with these fun place mats. Perfect for a round table, the circular opening is easily created by turning back the bias edges of folded triangles that surround a square of print fabric.

MATERIALS

Yardage is based on 42"-wide fabric and is sufficient to make 4 placemats.

2⅞ yards of gray dot print for background, backing, and binding
8" x 8" square *each* of 4 assorted prints
1 yard of 45"-wide batting or 2 yards of 20"-wide heavyweight interfacing*

** I used CRAF-TEX Plus interfacing from Bosal, which is fusible on both sides. You can also use precut round place mats from Bosal.*

CUTTING

From the batting or interfacing, cut:
4 circles, 16" in diameter (see "Make a Circle Pattern" below)

From the gray dot print, cut:
2 strips, 3¾" x 42"; crosscut into 16 squares, 3¾" x 3¾"
3 strips, 3½" x 42"; crosscut into:
 4 rectangles, 3½" x 13½"
 4 rectangles, 3½" x 8"
3 strips, 6" x 42"; crosscut into:
 4 rectangles, 6" x 16"
 4 rectangles, 6" x 8"
4 circles, 16" in diameter

From the *bias* of the remaining gray dot print, cut:
Enough 2¼"-wide strips to make a 240"-long strip when pieced together

Make a Circle Pattern

If you don't have a compass that can make a 16" circle, try this method. You'll need a 17" square of paper and a piece of string about 12" long. Fold the paper square into quarters and crease the folds to mark the center; unfold the square. Tie the string around a short pencil and then insert a pin through the string 8" from the pencil. Place the pin through the paper at the center point. Keeping the string taut and the pencil straight, draw the circle.

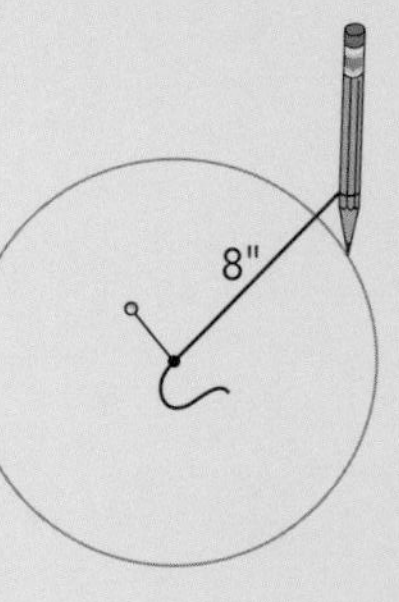

ASSEMBLING THE PLACE MATS

Sew with right sides together using a ¼" seam allowance.

1. Refer to "Baste the Backing and Batting Together" (page 68) to attach a batting or interfacing circle to the wrong side of each backing circle using your favorite method.

2. Draw two lines perpendicular to each other, 3" from the outer edges of a batting or interfacing circle as shown. Lay an assorted-print 8" square right side up on the batting circle, lining up two adjacent sides with the drawn lines; pin in place. Repeat with the remaining batting/backing circles.

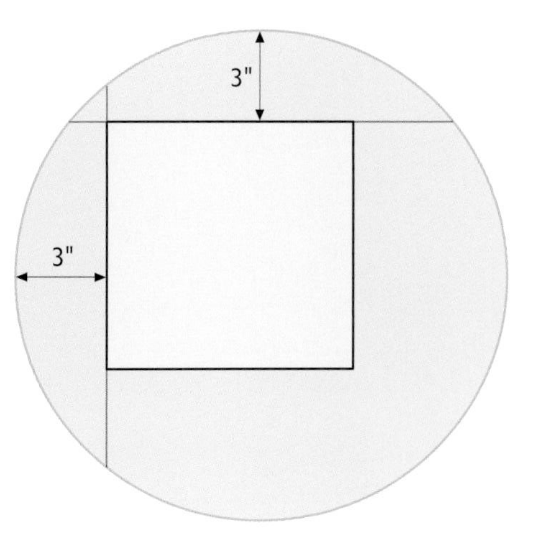

3. Press each gray 3¾" square in half diagonally, wrong sides together, to make a folded triangle. Lay a folded triangle in each corner of the squares you positioned in step 2. Pin each triangle in place, keeping the pins out of the seam allowances.

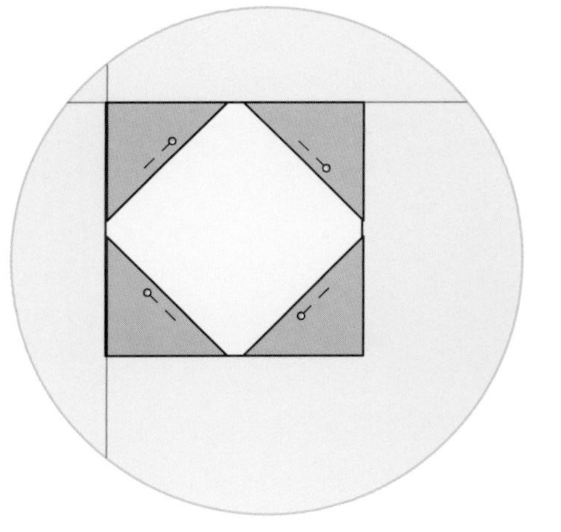

4. Lay a gray 3½" x 8" rectangle on top of one of the squares, right sides together, with the rectangle edges aligned with the top edge of the squares. Pin, and then sew through all the layers. Press the rectangle open.

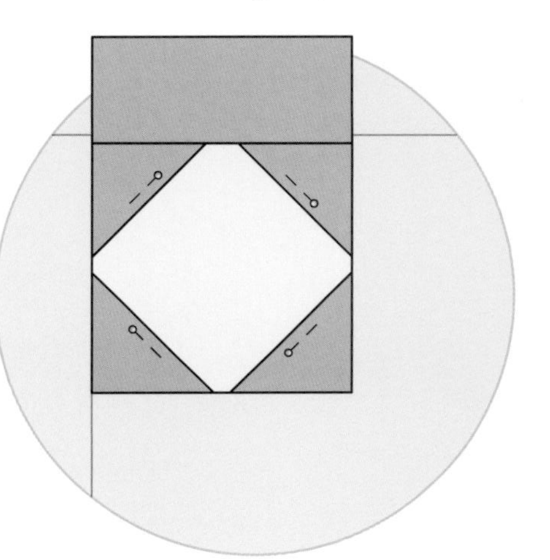

5. Sew a gray 6" x 8" rectangle to the bottom edge of the square. Press the rectangle open.

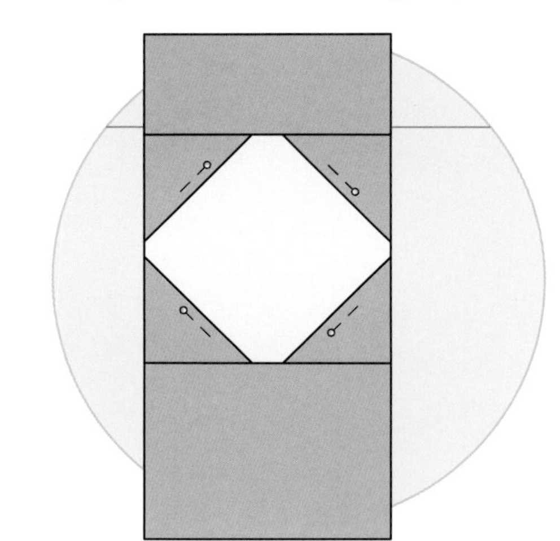

6. Pin a gray 3½" x 13½" rectangle to the left edge of the sewn unit, aligning the raw edges and positioning the rectangle so the circle will be covered when the rectangle is pressed open. Sew the rectangle in place, and then press it open.

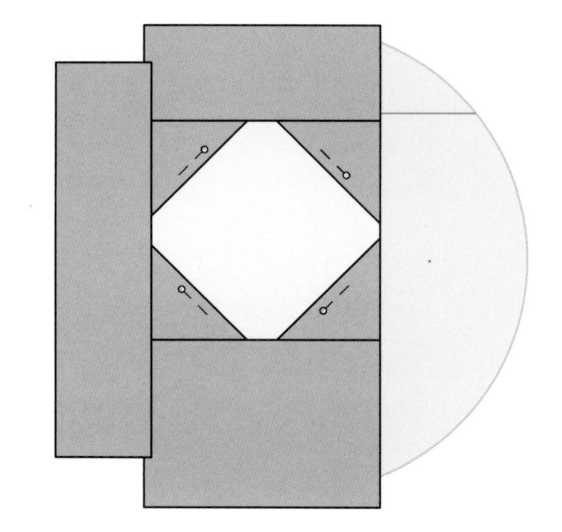

7. Pin a gray 6" x 16" rectangle to the right edge of the sewn unit, aligning the raw edges and positioning the rectangle so the circle will be covered when the rectangle is pressed open. Sew the rectangle in place, and then press it open.

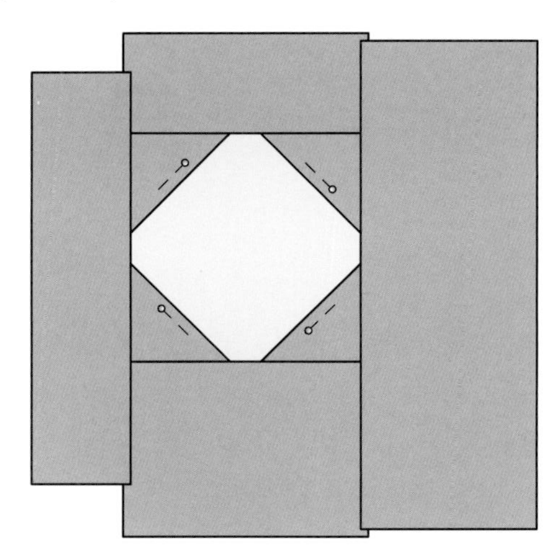

8. Flip the place mat over and trim the excess gray fabric to the same size as the backing and batting.

9. Repeat steps 4–8 with the remaining batting/backing sandwiches.

FINISHING

1. Remove the pins from all of the folded triangles. Refer to "Creating the Illusion of Curves" (page 75) to turn back the folded edge of each triangle to create a curve and edgestitch it in place.

2. Refer to "Binding" (page 76) to join the gray bias strips into one long strip and use it to bind the edges of each place mat.

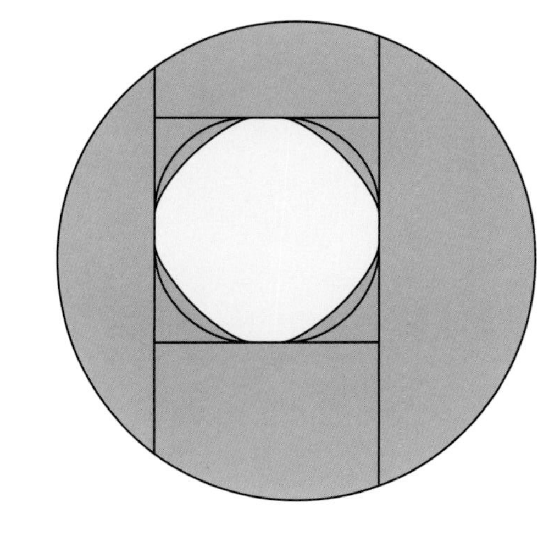

Lazy River
BED RUNNER

FINISHED BED RUNNER: 28½" x 82½" (full/queen)

Using a runner is a quick and beautiful way to enhance a bed covering. This scrappy version starts with pieced rectangles that are quickly transformed into "canoe" shapes with the addition of folded kite-shaped pieces placed in each corner.

MATERIALS

Yardage is based on 42"-wide fabric.

2⅞ yards of white solid for background and border
14 fat eighths (9" x 21") of assorted blue and brown prints for pieced units
½ yard of dark-blue print for binding
1⅞ yards of fabric for backing
30" x 84" piece of batting

CUTTING

From *each* of the assorted blue and brown prints, cut:
1 strip, 6½" x 21"; crosscut into 6 rectangles, 3½" x 6½" (84 total)

From the white solid, cut:
1 strip, 24½" x 42"; crosscut into 11 rectangles, 2½" x 24½"
5 strips, 2½" x 42"
40 kite pieces (pattern on page 65)

From the dark-blue print, cut:
6 strips, 2½" x 42"

ASSEMBLING THE BED RUNNER

Sew with right sides together using a ¼" seam allowance.

1. Randomly select eight assorted blue and brown 3½" x 6½" rectangles and sew them together along the long edges to make a pieced unit. Press the seam allowances in one direction. Repeat to make a total of 10 units.

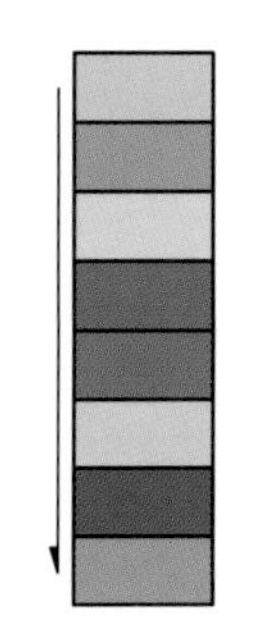

Make 10.

2. From the backing fabric, make a piece approximately 30" x 84". Refer to "Baste the Backing and Batting Together" (page 68) to attach the batting to the wrong side of the pieced backing rectangle using your favorite method.

3. Draw lines on the batting through the vertical and horizontal centers to mark the rectangle center. Draw two more lines, parallel to and 12¼" from each side of the vertical center line as shown below.

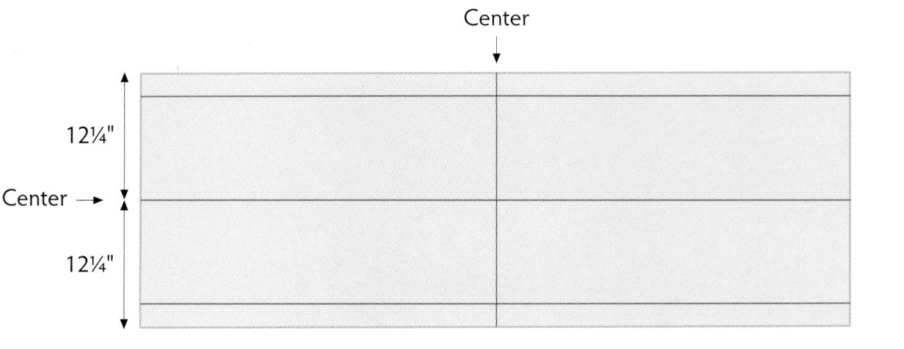

4. Press each white kite shape in half along the fold line, wrong sides together, to make a folded triangle. Pin a folded triangle to each corner of the pieced units from step 1, aligning the triangle raw edges with the pieced-unit raw edges.

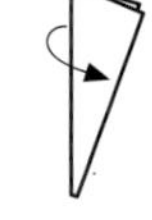

Fold and press.

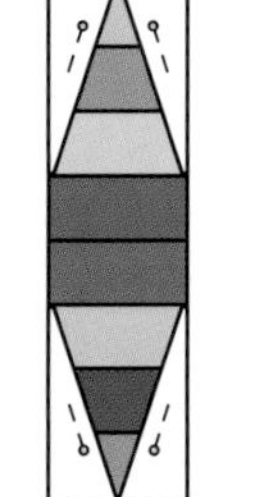

5. Center a white 2½" x 24½" rectangle on the horizontal center line of the batting, right side up. Place a prepared pieced unit from step 4 over the rectangle and pin it in place along the right edge of the rectangle. Sew the pieces together through all the layers. Press the pieced unit open. Repeat to add a pieced unit to the left edge of the white rectangle. Do not remove the pins yet.

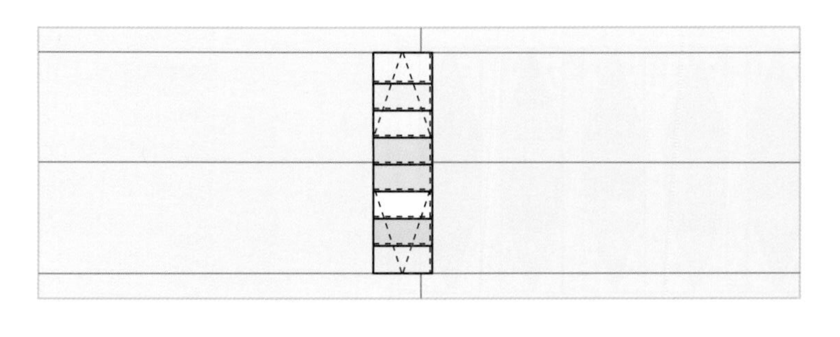

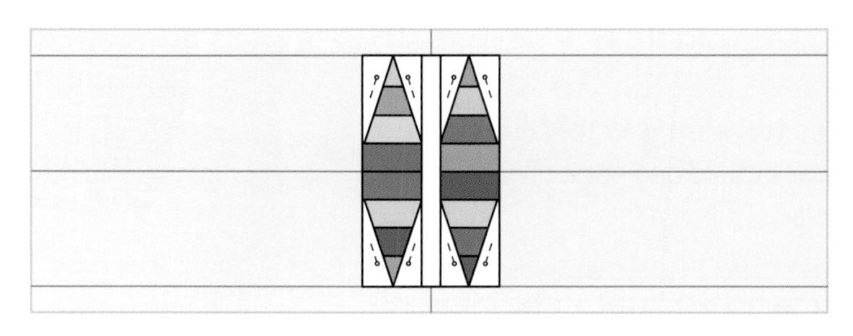

6. Pin a white 2½" x 24½" rectangle to the long raw edges of each of the pieced units on the batting/backing sandwich and stitch them in place. Press the rectangles open.

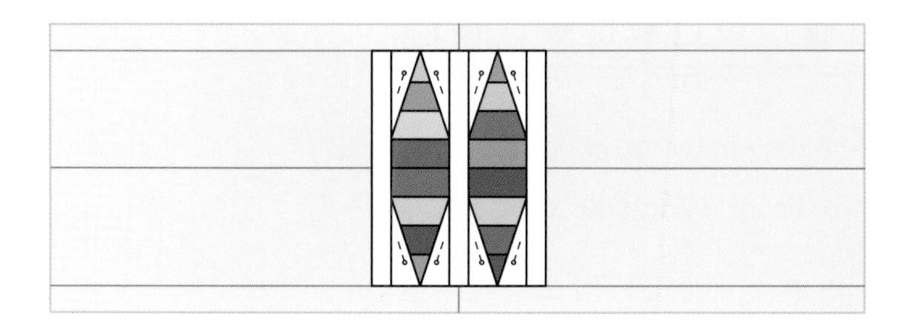

7. Continue adding pieced units and then white rectangles to the batting/backing sandwich until all of the pieces are stitched in place.

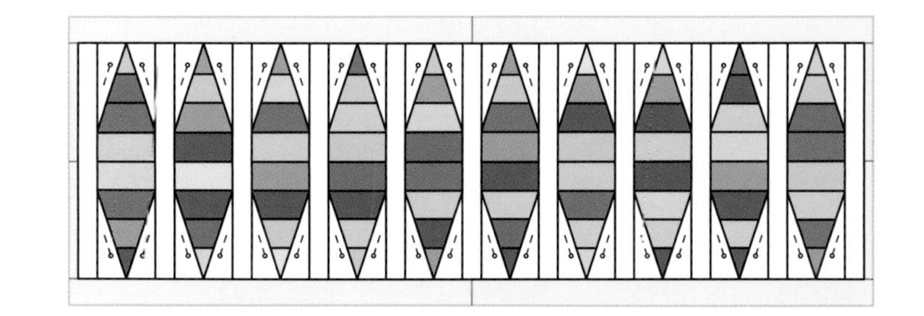

The Quilt-As-You-Go Method

All the projects in this book are made using the quilt-as-you-go method. For this method, you start with your backing and batting basted together, and then stitch the pieces for the project top through all the layers of the sandwich. The result is that you're quilting your project at the same time you're piecing it. This method is somewhat like paper piecing, with your batting/backing sandwich acting like the foundation, but in this case your patchwork pieces are precut and you're working from the front rather than the back.

Read Those Instructions

Be sure to read all of the instructions completely before beginning a project. The preparations might differ a little bit from one project to another. After reading through the entire project, read through each step again before beginning.

WHAT YOU'LL NEED

The tools and supplies you need for the quilt-as-you-go method are basically the same as what you use for traditional piecing, it's just the method that's different. That being said, here's a basic overview of what you'll need, as well as some of my favorites.

FABRIC. For best results, use 100% cotton fabrics for your projects, preferably quilt-shop-quality cottons. I like to use prints rather than solid colors or tone-on-tone prints for my quilt backing because the stitches will show through on the back. A print helps hide the stitches better.

BATTING. You can use batting made from any fiber you like. What's more important to consider is the thickness and how the batting is constructed. The loftier and more loosely constructed the batting is, the harder it is to work with for this technique. I've tried a lot of products and prefer to use fusible fleece (a dense, low-loft polyester batting with a fusible adhesive on one side) from Bosal. Bosal carries two thicknesses; I find that the lighter-weight one is perfect for runners and toppers, while the slightly thicker one is great for baby quilts. Fusible batting or fleece is ideal for quilting as you go. You simply iron your backing fabric to the adhesive side of the batting, and then you can get started sewing right away.

INTERFACING. For some projects, like the "Let's Dish Place Mats" (page 6), a stiff, heavyweight, double-sided fusible interfacing will give you less drape than batting will.

BASTING TOOL. If your batting or interfacing isn't fusible, you'll need to use another method to keep the backing and batting together while you sew the top pieces to the sandwich. Basting spray, quilter's safety pins, and thread are all good options. If you use basting spray, make sure it's a temporary bond so it allows you to reposition the fabric if needed and won't gum up your needle when you sew through it.

CLEAR ACRYLIC RULER. Use the same rulers you use for rotary cutting your fabrics to mark placement lines on your batting and fabrics. For some techniques, you'll need a ruler with the 45° angle marked.

MARKING PEN OR PENCIL. I like to use a water-soluble pen, a chalk pencil, or a pencil with a light-colored marking substance that won't show through light-colored fabrics to mark lines on the batting and fabric. In some cases a regular pen or marker with nontoxic ink works fine as long as you're marking cutting lines that will be cut away, or your fabrics are dark enough for the ink not to show through them or be visible if the ink should bleed into them.

IRON AND IRONING BOARD. You'll need these for adhering fusible batting to the backing, as well as for pressing each piece after it's been stitched to the batting/backing sandwich.

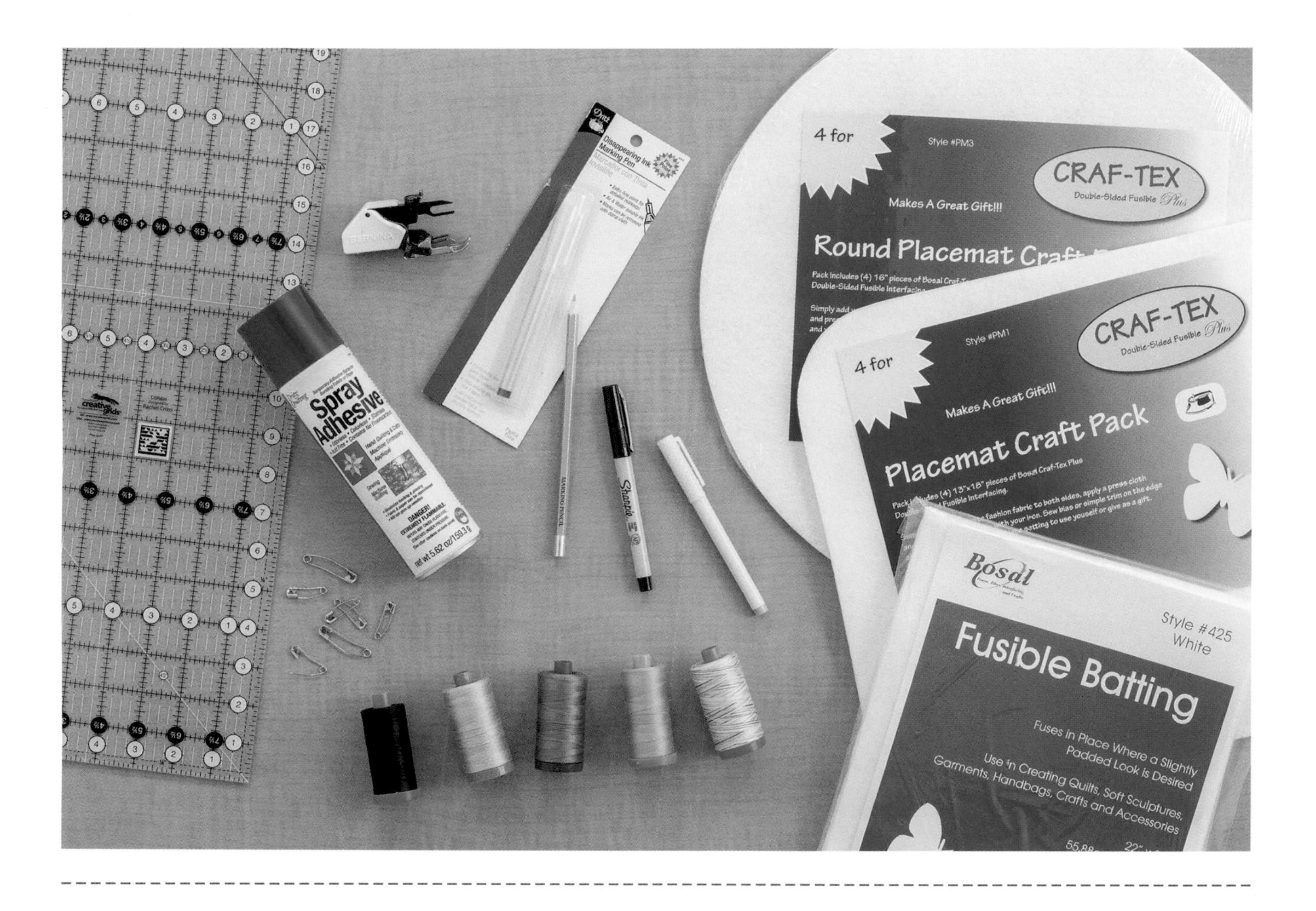

Some of the products I use for the quilt-as-you-go process

PAPER-BACKED FUSIBLE WEB. Appliqué projects require a lightweight, paper-backed fusible web that you can sew through.

SEWING MACHINE. For the quilt-as-you-go method, all you need is a machine that can sew a straight stitch. If you want to add appliqués to your project, you might want to use a blanket stitch, zigzag stitch, or another decorative stitch, although a straight stitch will also get the job done.

THREAD. Use your favorite cotton thread in a color that matches your backing fabric for the bobbin, because those stitches will be visible on the back. You can use whatever color you like for the top, but I usually prefer to use the same color for both the top and bobbin so that the top thread won't peek through on the backing. My favorite piecing thread is Aurifil Mako 50-weight 2-ply thread. It's great-quality thread, and it comes in a variety of colors.

WALKING FOOT OR EVEN-FEED FOOT. Unlike typical patchwork where you'd use a ¼" patchwork presser foot, for this method you'll want to use a walking foot or even-feed foot for the best results. If your machine didn't come with either of these feet, check with your dealer or see if a generic walking foot will fit your machine. This type of presser foot helps feed the top fabric through the machine just like the feed dogs do for the bottom fabric, which is crucial to prevent fabrics from shifting, sliding, and wrinkling when sewing through the layers of fabric and batting. If you don't have one of these presser feet, use a very thin batting and pin the pieces securely onto the batting before sewing.

QUILT-AS-YOU-GO BASICS

Every technique starts with knowing the basics. Once you understand the basic method of building your backing-and-batting sandwich and applying strips to it, we'll delve into working with triangles, filling areas with strips that go in different directions, adding appliqués and dimensional embellishments, and sewing curves.

Prepare the Pieces

Cut the pieces according to the project instructions. For some projects, you'll be ready to start the quilt-as-you-go process with the pieces as you've cut them. For others, like "Stacked Lanterns Table Runner" (page 16), you'll need to preassemble some pieces before you can begin stitching the pieces to the batting/backing sandwich.

Prepare the Backing

Cut the backing about 2" larger than the finished quilt and approximately the same size as the batting. Many of the projects in this book are small enough that you can cut the backing from a single width of the fabric, while others will instruct you to piece the fabric to create a backing the required size. Piecing the backing will let you get by with purchasing the least amount of fabric. If you prefer to avoid a pieced backing, just make sure to purchase enough fabric to include the additional 1" required on each side of the quilt.

Baste the Backing and Batting Together

As mentioned earlier, you'll be sewing the quilt-top pieces to the batting and backing at the same time in order to have a completed quilt top when the piecing is finished. To do this, you first need to baste the backing and batting together. There are several ways you can do this, but for all of the methods, make sure there aren't any puckers or wrinkles on the backing before you begin piecing.

My preference is to use fusible batting or interfacing and fuse the pieces together. Follow the manufacturer's instructions for the correct heat setting and fusing time. I've found that using steam speeds up the fusing process, but if the product instructions don't specifically call for using steam, try it on a test "sandwich" before using it in your project.

For nonfusible batting, I like to use basting spray to attach the batting/interfacing to the backing. Follow the manufacturer's instructions to spray one side of the batting with the basting spray, and then place the wrong side of the backing piece over the sprayed side of the batting, and smooth it out with your hands.

You can also pin baste your backing to the batting using quilter's safety pins or hand baste the layers together using basting thread. These methods take quite a bit longer than the fusible method, and you have to be a little more careful about the back puckering. They work well, though, if you don't have access to fusible products or basting sprays. Safety pins need to be removed when you reach them; thread-basting stitches should be removed after the piecing is finished and before the binding is applied.

Mark the Batting

Once the backing and batting or interfacing are basted together, you'll need to mark some lines on the batting to use as a guide for placing the fabric pieces. Each project specifies how to mark the batting. Use a clear ruler and a marking pen or pencil (refer to "What You'll Need" on page 66) to mark accurate lines that are easy to see.

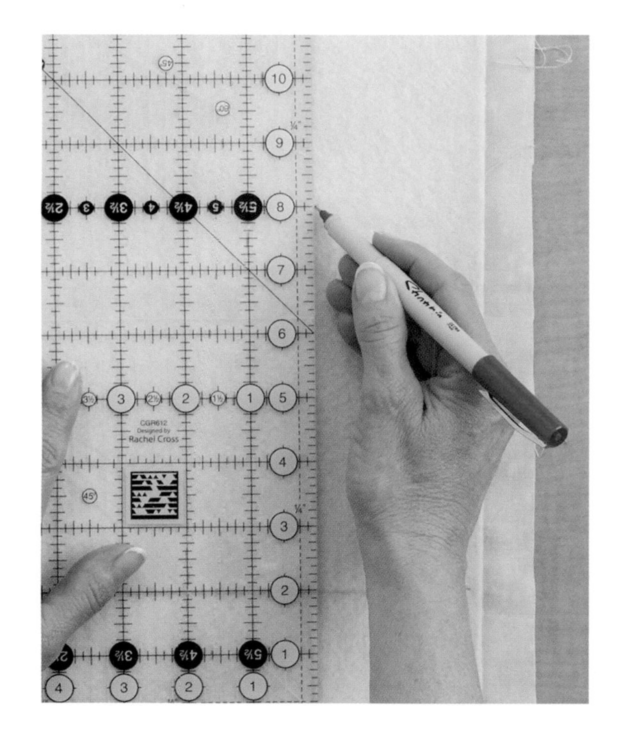

Prepare to Sew

Use a scant ¼" seam allowance for all of the projects unless otherwise noted. Attach the walking foot or even-feed foot to your machine and check the accuracy of your seam allowance before you begin; make adjustments if needed. Many of the projects in this book are very forgiving, so an accurate seam allowance isn't always required, but it can make a difference in finished sizes if not used.

At the beginning and end of each seam, sew a few stitches in the same spot to secure the threads. Many newer machines have a "tie off" button or "fix" button that you can press, and the machine does this automatically. There's no need to backstitch, because your seams will always overlap ¼", but taking just a few stitches in the same spot will allow you to trim threads close to the surface on the back of the quilt.

Shifty Layers

If you're using a walking foot and still feel like the fabrics are shifting, try releasing the presser-foot pressure a little bit.

Piece the Top

Your pieces are cut, the backing and batting are basted together, and your machine is ready to sew. It's time to quilt as you go!

1. Place the first piece right side up on the batting where instructed, using the lines on the batting as a guide.

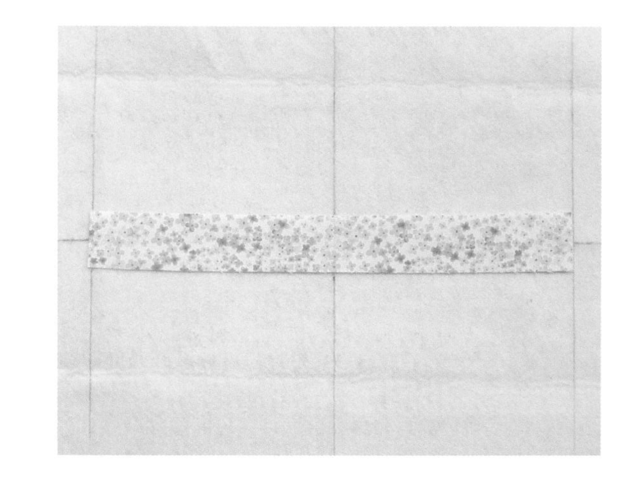

2. Position the next piece over the first strip, right sides together, aligning the raw edges along the edge indicated in the project instructions. Pin the pieces together.

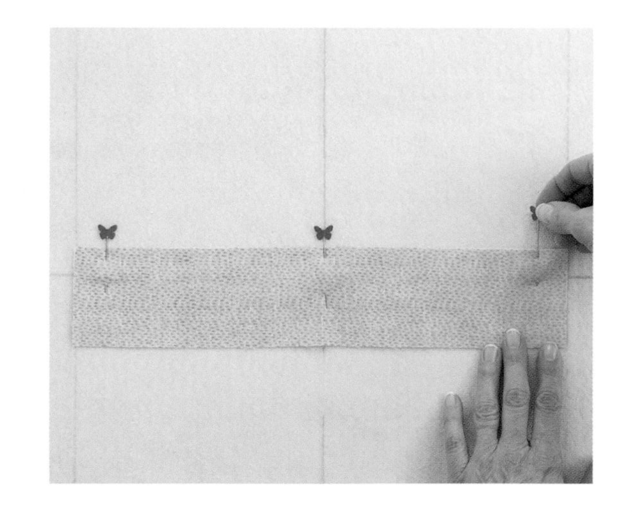

3. Using a ¼" seam allowance, sew through all the layers, remembering to lock your stitches at the beginning and end of the seamline.

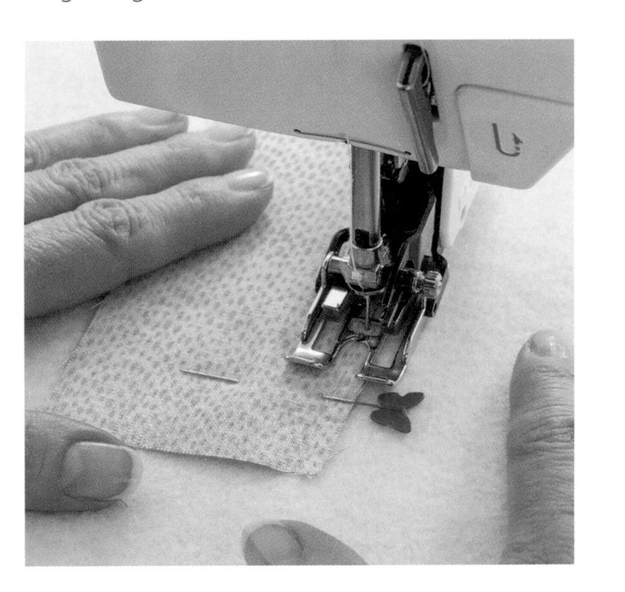

4. With your fingers, open the second piece to the right side and finger-press the seam. Then use an iron to press the unit. Try to avoid directly touching the iron to the batting so as not to melt it. For some projects I simply finger-press each piece as I sew, and then press with an iron after I've completed a full row. Use your best judgment and go to the iron if you feel like your pieces aren't lying flat with just finger-pressing.

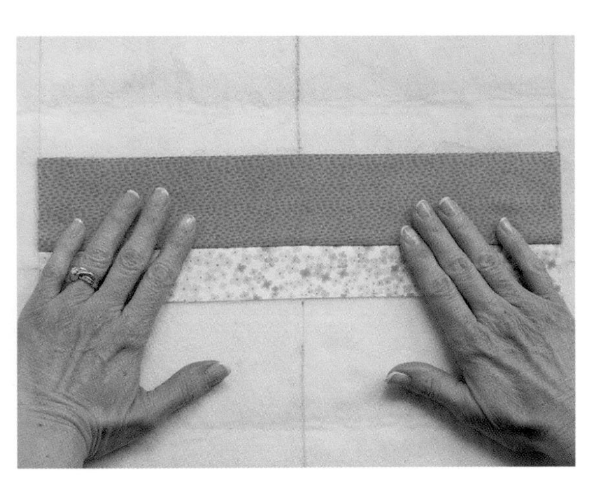

5. Lay the next piece in place as directed in the project instructions and pin it in place. Sew through all the layers, and press as before.

Continue in this manner until all the pieces have been added.

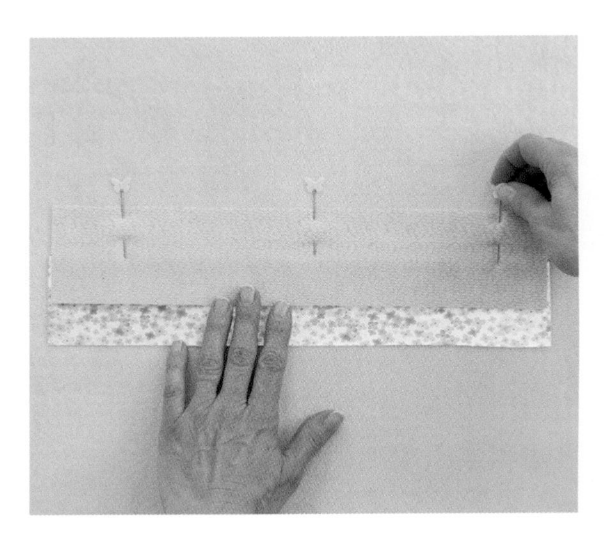

TACKLING TRIANGLES

By now you've seen that adding strips, squares, and rectangles with the quilt-as-you-go method is pretty easy to do. But sometimes a quilter wants to add triangles to the design. Adding triangles requires a more precise seam allowance and careful sewing than adding strips, squares, and rectangles, but the results can be spectacular! When sewing triangles in regular piecing, you can always flip your block over to see if your seam is accurate and to be sure you're not cutting off the triangle points. Because you can't do that with this technique, I'll show you some other tricks that will help you be successful.

When it's time to add a triangle to your project, have a ruler handy that has an easy-to-see ¼" line as well as a 45° diagonal line marked on it. Then grab a favorite marking tool that's either erasable or won't show through your fabrics. Follow the step-by-step sequence below to add triangles to corners (see "Sienna Sunrise Topper" on page 20) or to a straight setting (see "Winging It Table Runner" on page 24).

Adding Triangles to Corners

This process starts by adding other pieces to the batting/backing sandwich first. The example shown and referred to here is from "Sienna Sunrise Topper." The black center rectangle and yellow rectangles surrounding it have already been stitched in place, and the triangles will be added across the corners of the black rectangle.

1. With the 45° angle of the ruler aligned with the short side of the center rectangle seam, align the 1/4" line of the ruler with the corner of the center rectangle. Draw the placement line across the yellow surrounding rectangles.

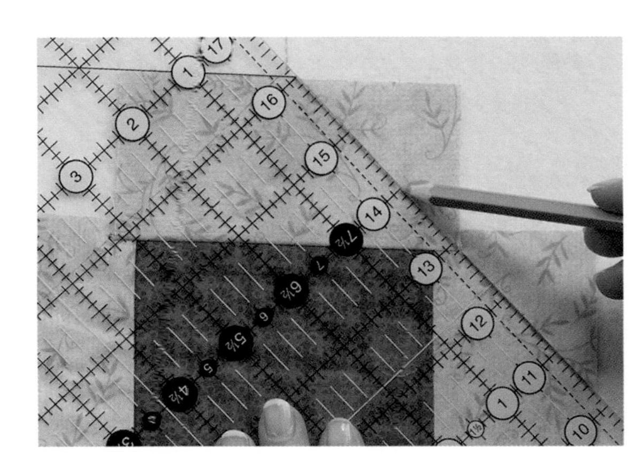

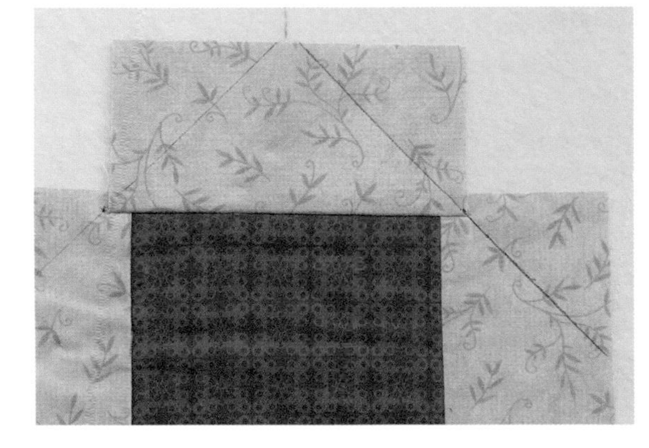

2. Align the triangle long edge with the drawn line, right sides together, and pin in place.

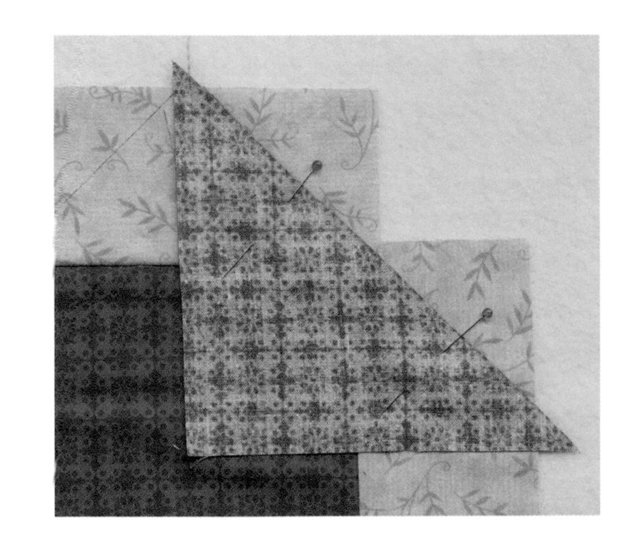

3. Sew along the edge of the triangle using an accurate 1/4" seam allowance. Trim the yellow fabric that will be under the triangle when it's pressed open even with the long edge of the triangle.

Mark Your Placement

The short edges of the triangle should be in line with the outer edges of the other pieces. However, when adding bias-edge triangles during the quilt-as-you-go process, there will be instances where your triangles won't line up 100% accurately. If a triangle is a little off, as shown in the photo below, simply use your ruler to draw a placement line for the next set of strips or rectangles and use that instead of the edge of the fabrics to place your next piece.

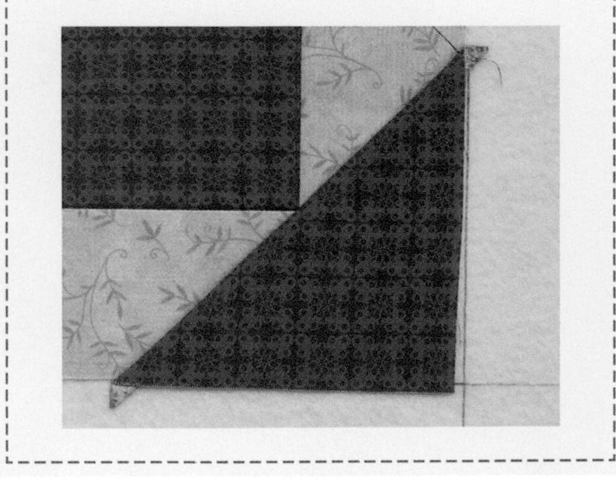

4. Press the triangle open, taking care to avoid the exposed batting with the hot iron.

Adding Triangles to a Straight Setting

This process also starts by adding other pieces to the batting/backing sandwich first. The example shown and referred to here is from "Winging It Table Runner" (page 24). The center diamond and white rectangles surrounding it have already been stitched in place, and the triangles will be added across the side points of the diamond.

1. Mark lines parallel to and ¼" from the top and bottom points of the diamond, using the original horizontal center line for alignment. Align the ¼" line of the ruler across a side point of the diamond, using the horizontal marked lines to make sure the ruler is completely perpendicular. Mark the placement line.

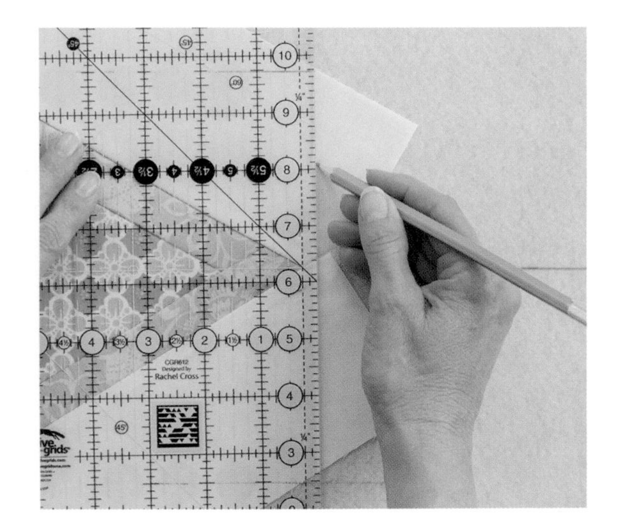

2. Center the triangle along the drawn line, right sides together, and sew ¼" from the edge of the triangle. Trim the fabric that sticks out beyond the seam allowance so it's even with the triangles edges.

SEWING BY NUMBERS

This isn't like painting by numbers, where you put certain colors in certain areas. This method is really just filling in designated areas with pieces in a particular order. You have to fill in one area before you can start the next. You're using the marked batting pretty much like a foundation, so if you've ever done any foundation piecing, you'll notice a similarity. The main difference is that you're working from the drawn side of the "foundation."

Mark the Batting

After attaching the backing to your batting, draw your pattern onto the batting. This is usually just straight lines or boxes, so to do this you'll need a fairly long ruler and a marking tool. I like to use a permanent pen to make sure the lines don't disappear halfway through the project. Just be aware that if you're using very light fabrics, you need to make sure that the markings won't show through them.

Follow the instructions for each project to draw the lines and numbers on the batting. Make sure lines extend 1" to 2" past the point where they intersect. The numbers indicate the order in which to fill each area.

Fill In Areas

You can use whole or pieced strips with this method, and they can be all the same width or different widths. Unless the pattern specifies to cut strips to a certain length, start with full width-of-fabric strips and trim them to the lengths needed as you go until the strip is too short to cover an area.

1. Start by filling area 1. Lay a strip, right side up, where indicated for the project. For "Stripalicious Table Runner" (page 30) you'll start on one edge, and for "Spring Bouquet Wall Hanging" (page 33) you'll start in the center. Trim the strip to the appropriate length so it extends beyond the drawn lines by at least ¼". Lay another strip on top of the first strip, right sides together, and trim it so it extends beyond the drawn lines by at least ½". Pin and then sew the strip in place. Press the strip open. Keep adding strips to the area, either on one side of the first strip or on both sides, depending on the project instructions, until the area is about halfway filled. Lay your ruler over the pieced area, with the ¼" line on the ruler aligned with the marked line on the batting. Draw a line on the strips, marking the placement line for the next area. Repeat for any remaining sides where the strips cross the lines on the batting.

2. Continue to add strips to area 1 until it is completely filled. Lay the ruler back on the pieced area, lining up the ¼" line on the ruler with the extended lines of the area. Mark the line on the strips, extending the line you previously marked at the halfway point.

3. Fill in area 2 next. Lay the first strip right side down, with the raw edge aligned with the placement line. Trim the strip so it extends at least ¼" past the adjacent drawn lines; pin and then stitch it in place. If your fabrics are light enough to see through, trim the ends of the strips from area 1 even with the edge of the strip so they won't show through when you press the strip open. Press the strip open. Continue filling this area in the same manner as area 1.

4. Work in numerical order to fill all of the remaining areas in the same manner as areas 1 and 2.

Binding

Binding the edges is the last step before your project is finished. I prefer to use a double-fold binding technique for all my quilt-as-you-go projects. Straight-grain strips cut across the width of the fabric can be used for projects with straight edges, but projects with curved edges, like the "Scraptastic Coasters" (page 9), will require bias-cut strips in order to go around the curves smoothly. The only difference in the two types of binding is how you cut and join the strips. For either type of binding, the project instructions will tell you the number of strips to cut.

STRAIGHT-GRAIN BINDING

I cut my strips 2½" wide, which is the width indicated in the project instructions. If you prefer a different width, just be sure to adjust the overlap amount when you join the ends.

1. Cut binding strips across the width of the fabric, from selvage to selvage.
2. Sew the binding strips together using a diagonal seam to create one long strip. Trim the excess, leaving a ¼" seam allowance. Press the seam allowances open.

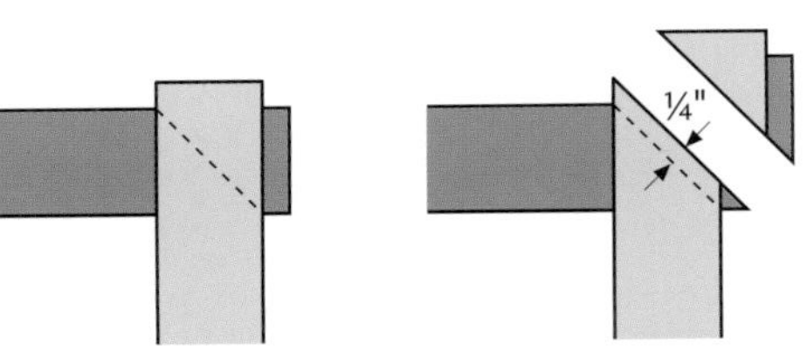

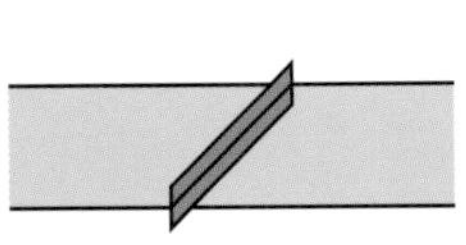

Press seam allowances open.

3. Fold the strip in half lengthwise, wrong sides together; press.
4. Place the beginning of the binding strip at about the center of one side of the quilt top, aligning the raw edges. Using a walking foot or even-feed foot and a ¼" seam allowance, begin sewing the binding to the quilt, leaving about 8" of the binding free. Backstitch at the beginning of the seam to secure it. Continue stitching to the corner of the quilt, stopping ¼" from the edge. Backstitch, and then clip the threads and remove the quilt from the machine.

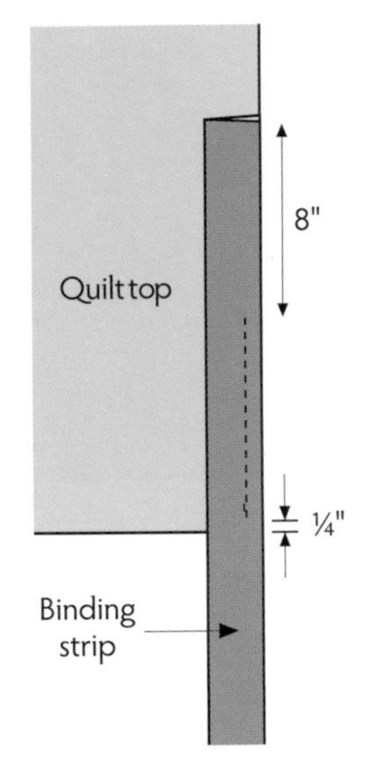

5. Rotate the quilt counterclockwise a quarter turn. Fold the binding up and away from the quilt so the strip is aligned with the side of the quilt and the fold forms a 45° angle. Holding the fold in place, fold the binding back onto the quilt to form a fold parallel with the upper edge of the quilt. Begin stitching again at the top edge of the quilt; backstitch, and then continue sewing until you are ¼" from the next corner. Backstitch, and then clip the threads and remove the quilt from the machine. Repeat for all of the remaining corners.

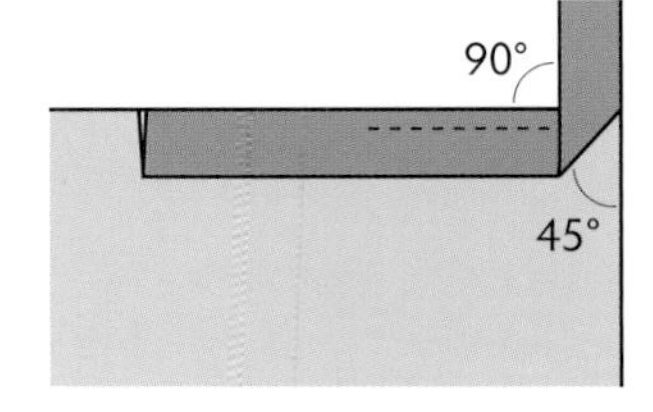

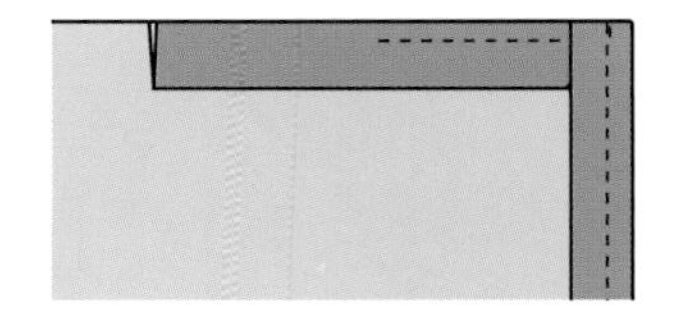

6. When you are within approximately 10" from where you began, stop stitching; backstitch.

7. Lap the end of the binding strip over the beginning of the binding strip. Trim the top end so it overlaps the bottom end 2½" (or the width of the binding strip).

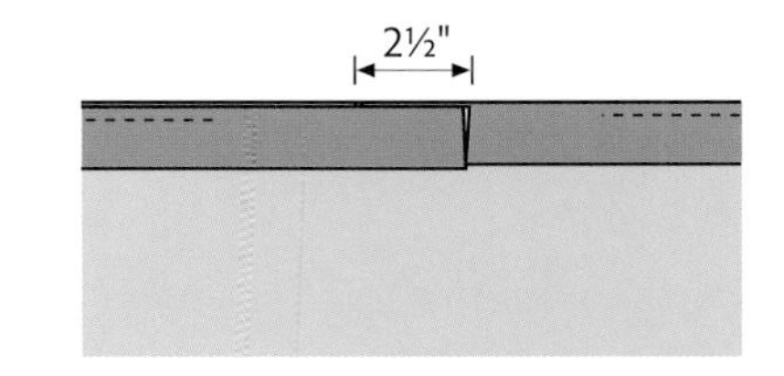

8. Open both ends of the binding and align them right sides together at right angles. Draw a diagonal line from corner to corner as shown; pin the strips together.

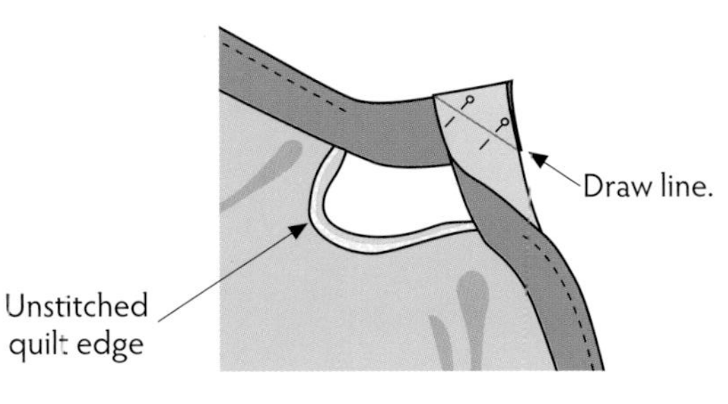

9. Stitch on the drawn line. Check to be sure you've sewn the ends together correctly and that the binding fits the quilt top. Trim the seam allowances to ¼" and press them open.

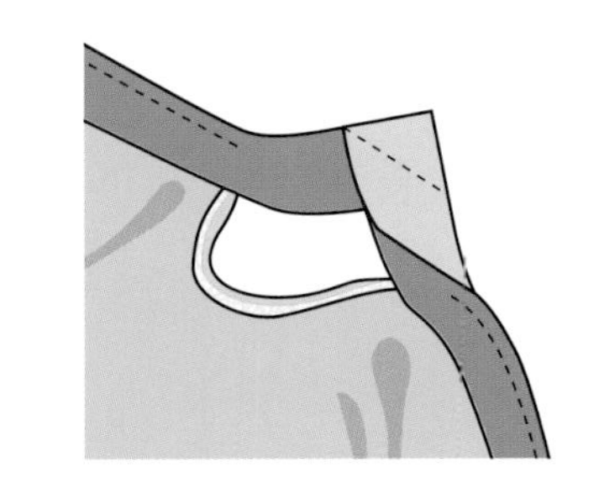

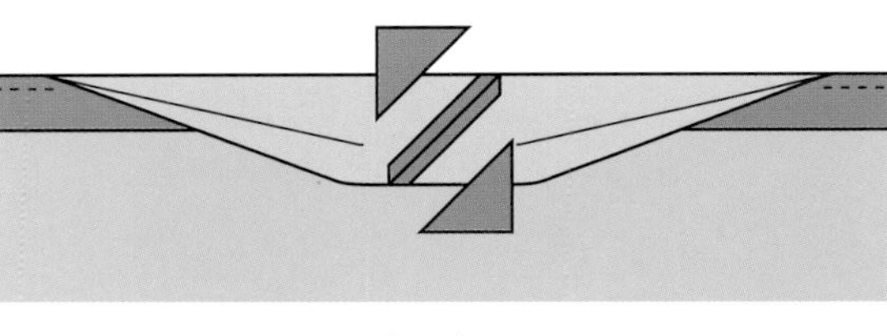

Trim to ¼" and press open.

10. Refold the binding and finish stitching it to the quilt.

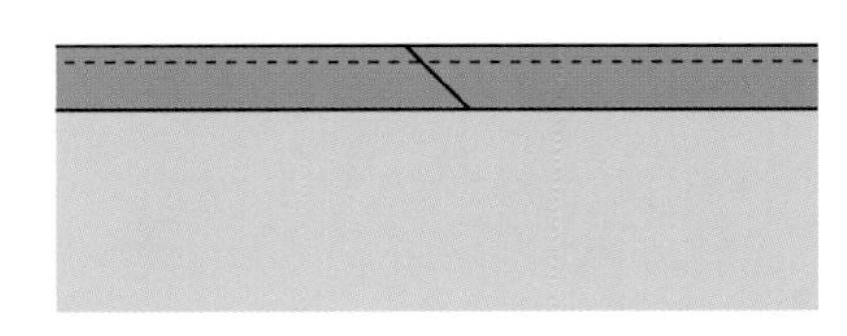

11. Fold the binding to the back of the quilt and stitch it in place, mitering the corners.

BIAS BINDING

The "Scraptastic Coasters" are small, so I reduced the width of the binding to 2¼" to achieve a smoother finished edge.

1. Lay the binding fabric on the cutting surface in a single layer. Align the 45° line of your ruler with one of the selvage edges. Cut along the ruler edge to make the first cut. Using the first cut as a guide, cut strips to the width indicated in the project instructions.

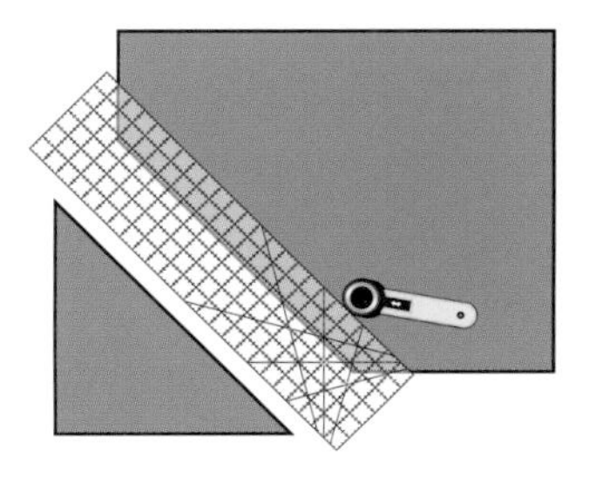

2. To join the strips, place the ends of two strips right sides together as shown. The corners will extend about ¼" on each side, creating a V. Stitch between the two Vs. Press the seam allowances open, and trim to ¼" if needed. Join the remaining strips in the same manner to make one long strip.

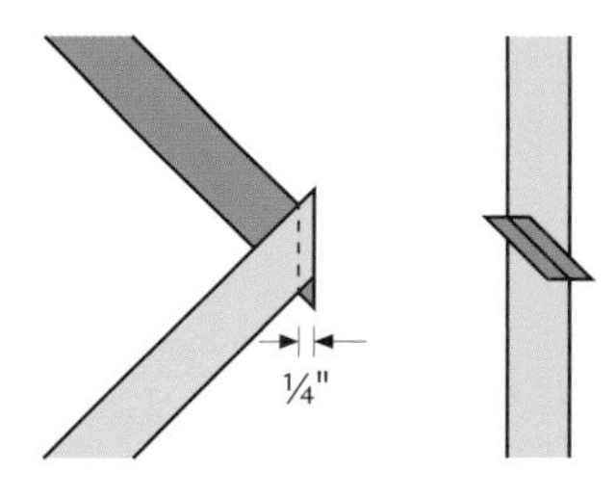

Press seam allowances open.

3. Refer to steps 3–11 of "Straight-Grain Binding" on page 76 to attach the binding to the quilt edges.

Tucked Ends

When your quilt is really small or doesn't have long enough straight edges, it's sometimes hard to sew the two ends together to finish your binding. In these cases I use the tucked-ends method. Piece and prepare the binding strips the same way as for straight-grain binding. After pressing the strip in half, unfold one end and trim it at an angle (either 45° or 60°). Press under the angled end ¼" and refold the binding strip. Sew the binding to the quilt as described for straight-grain binding, beginning about 2" from the angled end. When you reach your starting point, trim the end of the binding strip so it can be tucked inside the angled end. Once it's tucked in, finish sewing the binding to the project.

Acknowledgments

A book like this would not be possible without the help of many caring people, whether it is because of their wonderful encouragement and inspiration or their hard work and attention to detail. I would like to send my deepest gratitude to the following individuals for making me look so good:

I have to start with my right-hand, right-brain sanity saver and soundboard, Yvonne Geske. Thank you for your sewing skills, pattern-testing skills, attention to detail, and all the laughs and good times, as well as for putting up with me and my quirks in general. Thank you for making the "Stacked Lanterns Table Runner" and the "Winging It Table Runner" projects for this book.

My kids, Atli, Gisli, and Svana, for all of your support and inspiration. Thank you for understanding when mom is buried in the sewing studio or in front of the computer and for picking up the slack on household chores or making dinner. I love you more than anything.

My family in Iceland. Thank you for supporting me through thick and thin and always having my back. It's hard being so far away, but love crosses oceans easily and I feel your presence every day.

Big thanks to the professional staff at Martingale, starting with Karen Burns for talking me into this idea in the first place. Cathy Reitan, Karen Soltys, and Laurie Baker, thank you for your ever-so-professional and proficient work on this baby.

I would like to give big thanks to the following colleagues in the quilting industry. Your support is crucial with a project like this and your fast responses, generosity, and friendships make me feel like I can accomplish anything: Carol DeSousa, Anna Fishkin, Lissa Alexander, Rolando Berdion, Alex Veronelli, Nancy Jewell, Jina Barnes, Hayden Lees, and Cam Kilman.

Supplies/Resources

I would like to thank the following companies in the quilting industry for contributing wonderful materials used throughout the book.

Art Gallery Fabrics

Aurifil

Blend Fabrics

Bosal Foam & Fiber

Checker Distributors

Creative Grids

Moda Fabrics

Red Rooster Fabrics

Riley Blake Designs

Timeless Treasures Fabrics

Westminster Fabrics

About the Author

GUDRUN ERLA, the designer and owner of GE Designs, was born and raised in Iceland. She started quilting at the age of 23 and became totally addicted to it right away. She owned and ran quilt shops in her home country and designed patterns as well, until a career move brought her family to Minnesota in 2003. Since then Gudrun has been designing full-time and publishing patterns and books under her company name of GE Designs. Her numerous quilt-as-you-go patterns and books have been very popular among quiltmakers wanting to make quick quilted items for their homes or for gift giving.

Learn to Quilt-As-You-Go is Gudrun's first book with Martingale.